Emigrants in Chains

EMIGRANTS IN CHAINS

*A Social History of Forced Emigration
to the Americas of Felons, Destitute
Children, Political and Religious
Non-Conformists, Vagabonds,
Beggars and other
Undesirables
1607-1776*

Peter Wilson Coldham

Published by Genealogical Publishing Co., Inc.
1001 N. Calvert Street, Baltimore, Maryland 21202
Library of Congress Catalogue Card Number 91-76730
International Standard Book Number 0-8063-1329-3
Made in the United States of America

Extracts from Crown Copyright Documents are published
by permission of Her Majesty's Stationery Office

This is a revised and much enlarged treatment of the
"History of Transportation" which appeared as the
introductory volume in Mr. Coldham's nine-volume
Bonded Passengers to America, published in 1983.

Contents

Emigrants in Chains

Introduction

he transportation of convicted felons to remote and inhospitable frontier areas to expiate their offences by unremitting hard labour is a practice at least as old as the Roman Empire. Few colonising powers, however, can have relied so heavily and consistently on the wholesale deportation of their prison population as did England through two-and-a-half centuries of imperial expansion. By the time America made her Declaration of Independence in 1776, the prisons of England had disgorged some 50,000 of their inmates to the colonies, most of them destined to survive and, with their descendants, to populate the land of their exile. Within the space of their own lifetime some were able to achieve a freedom and status often denied them in their homeland, others used ill-gotten gains from their earlier exploits to buy freedom and a better life, while the majority were fated to remain tied to a form of serfdom which distinguished them little from bonded slaves.

Our history books have little or nothing to tell us about this great wave of dispossessed humanity nor of the significant part which forcible emigration played in the development of colonial America. Indeed, both statesmen and historians have often contrived to dismiss or minimise the scale of criminal transportation to the Americas. Thomas Jefferson gave it as his opinion in 1785 that

> the malefactors sent to America were not sufficient in number to merit enumeration [and] it was at a late period of their history that the practice began. I do not think the whole number would amount to 2,000 and, being principally men eaten up with disease, they married seldom and propagated little. I do not suppose that themselves and their descendants at present number 4,000.[1]

1

One of America's most distinguished historians committed himself to the verdict that

> some [early Virginians] were even convicts, but it must be remembered the crimes of which they were convicted were chiefly political. The number transported to Virginia for social crimes was never considerable.[2]

Another confided:

> Many transported convicts were victims of misfortune; and others were transported because they were married without the sanction of the Established Church. Many convicts were educated persons . . .[3]

Though neither opinion is wholly fallacious, both have conspired to minimise or impose a false gloss on the true nature and extent of England's trade in transported convicts which began in 1607 and came to an end only in 1851. This has remained for less partisan scholars to uncover.[4]

Those who were transported for offences ranging from petty theft to bigamy, infanticide and murder, were largely illiterate with neither the talent nor inclination to leave behind them a comprehensive record of their sufferings or later achievements. Those who transported them chose to ply their trade well away from the public stage where few questions were asked about their methods or profits. While the transportation agents could act as appointees of the Crown and of the law to perform what was perceived as a useful service by clearing the country of its undesirable population, small public interest was taken in the human misery and degradation that their activities caused. When William Wilberforce and other liberal spirits finally aroused the English conscience to the atrocities of the traffic in black slaves, the equally appalling brutality shown towards white slaves deported during the preceding two centuries was fading from memory — and the more closely regulated transportation schemes to Australia had yet to begin.[5]

Well before the new plantation in Virginia had come of age, a scheme had been worked out in England to reprieve from the gallows any whose crimes were less than murder, treason, rape, witchcraft, highway robbery, arson or burglary, in order that they might be shipped to the colony to "toyle in heavey and painefull workes." The supply of reprieved felons was maintained with little interruption throughout the seventeenth century despite growing opposition from the colonial Governors. The early years of the next century ushered in wars, internal rebellion and a severe economic decline, all of which gave rise to a sharp increase in lawlessness and prison populations. New measures were needed to dissipate and neutralise those felons who could not be disposed of by hanging, and in 1718 a new Act came into force whereby the sentence of seven years' transportation to the American colonies became the standard punishment for crimes other than the most trivial or most heinous; and even the sentence for murder, provided there were extenuating circumstances, could be commuted to a term of fourteen years or of a lifetime in the colonies.

During the last decade of British rule in mainland America, the London prison of Newgate and the prisons of the Home Counties were alone contributing over 500 felons each year as slave labour for the plantations to the enormous profit of the tobacco merchants who had a monopoly of the trade in human cargoes. Lest it be assumed that only the most vicious criminal elements were disposed of in this way, it is salutary to remark that by far the most prevalent offence for which the sentence of transportation was imposed was the theft of a handkerchief, though there is no escaping the fact that every shipload of felons sent to the plantations included its share of reprieved murderers, highwaymen and professional thieves.

Recruitment of labour to the American tobacco plantations and to domestic service of all kinds from schoolmastering to scullery work was achieved in very large measure through the emptying of English jails, workhouses, brothels and houses of correction. By such means the southern colonies acquired a reputation so dubious that it became increasingly difficult at home to attract new emigrants of standing or integrity. The popular view may be accurately judged from a propagandist publication written in 1656 by a certain John Hammond[6] who claimed to be drawing on his personal experience of twenty-one years in Virginia and Maryland. He was prepared to admit that

> the Country is reported to be an unhealthy place, a nest of Rogues, whores, desolate and rooking persons, a place of intolerable labour, bad usage and hard Diet . . . At the first settling, and many years after, it deserved most of these aspersions (nor were they then aspersions but truths). It was not settled at the publique charge; but when found out, challenged and maintained by Adventurers whose avarice and inhumanity brought in those inconveniencies which to this day brands Virginia. Then were jayls

emptied, youth seduced, infamous women drilled in, the provisions
all brought out from England . . . Complaints were repaied with
stripes, moneys with scoffs, tortures made delights and, in a word,
all and the worst that tyranny could inflict or act.

Having sketched in this frightful background, the author then attempted to allay his readers' fears by asserting, "Yet was not Virginia
all this while without divers honest and vertuous inhabitants." He
claimed, somewhat improbably:

> Theft is seldome punished as being seldome or never committed
> . . . Doors are nightly left open . . . yet I never heard of any
> losse ever received. I much pitty the dull stupidity of people
> necessitated in England who, rather than that they will remove
> themselves, live here a base, slavish, penurious life, as if there
> were a necessity to live and to live so, choosing rather than they
> will forsake England to stuff Newgate, Bridewell and other Jayles
> with their carkessies, nay cleave to Tyburn itself.

Even Hammond's extravagant enthusiasm was unable to disguise the
fact that limited freedom in England could often be exchanged by
the unwary for an indefinite slavery in Virginia, and he felt constrained
to append this caution:

> Let such as are so minded [to become planters] not rashly throw
> themselves upon the voyage, but observe the nature and enquire
> the qualities of the persons with whom they ingage to transport
> themselves.

He counselled them to procure contracts in writing before they left,

> for a promise signifies nothing . . . By a Law of the Country
> [i.e. Virginia], any one coming in and not paying their own
> passages must serve, if men and women, four years . . . The
> usual allowance for servants is, at their expiration [of service] a
> year's provision of corne, dubble apparrell, tooles necessary and
> land according to the custome of the Country, which is an old
> delusion for there is no land accustomary due to the servant, but
> to the Master; and therefore that Servant is unwise that will not
> dash out that custom in his covenant and make that due of land
> absolutely his own.

In truth there was little to distinguish the transported convict from the indentured servant once either had crossed the Atlantic. By the system of indentured service any person over the age of fifteen could bind himself over to a master or shipping merchant who, in return for giving him a free passage to America, could quite legally sell him into servitude in the plantations for a period of two to seven years. Significantly the very term "servant," as it was applied in the shipping trade of the time, made no distinction between convict and hired man.

Bristol, the principal English port of that time for emigration to America, despatched over 10,000 indentured servants westwards between 1654 and 1686.[7] Bristol merchants would take convicts or indentured servants indiscriminately and had little scruple as to how they were obtained. The trade was profitable and the merchants could well afford to ship their charges free because of the high prices obtainable for human labour at the port of delivery. So a trading pattern was set for a century and a half —an outward cargo of labourers to be exchanged for a return consignment of tobacco, both commodities in keen demand. A healthy but unskilled man would sell in America for as much as £10, while a skilled craftsman would fetch £25, and this at a time when the transatlantic passenger fare was reckoned at £4.

While it is impossible even to make an informed guess about the demographic balance of the southern colonies of America before the Revolutionary War, some indication of the effects of continuous convict transportation is conveyed in the following population statistics from Maryland in 1755:

> Free white males 50,695; free white females 47,662; male servants 4,625; female servants 2,246; male convicts 1,507; women convicts 386; boy convicts 67; girl convicts 21. The total of convicts still serving their sentence is 1,981.[8]

The pages which follow may not entirely vindicate Dr. Johnson's dictum of 1769 dismissing the population of North America as "a race of convicts [who] ought to be content with anything we allow them short of hanging,"[9] though they might lead to a re-interpretation of Sir William Blackstone's judgment:

> No power on earth except the authority of Parliament can send any subject of England out of the land against his will; no, not

even a criminal. For exile and transportation are punishments at present unknown to the common law; and, whenever the latter is now inflicted, it is either by the choice of the criminal himself to escape a capital punishment or else by the express direction of some modern Act of Parliament.[10]

NOTES

1. *Memoirs and Correspondence of Thomas Jefferson*, ed. T. J. Randolph (London, 1829), Vol. I, p. 406. Jefferson was commenting as American Minister in Paris on an article about the United States proposed for the French *Encyclopedia*.

2. George Bancroft, *A History of the United States of America* (New York, 1885), Vol. 1, p. 443.

3. Edward Channing, *A History of the United States of America* (New York, 1977), Vol. 2, p. 373.

4. Perhaps beginning with John Dunmore Lang in his book *Transportation and Colonization* (London, 1837), p. 38. He first quoted Jefferson's estimate and then correctly revised it to 50,000 for America as a whole.

5. The system of transportation as it affected Australia is outside the scope of this book and was finally discarded in 1851.

6. John Hammond, *Leah and Rachel or The Two Fruitful Sisters, Virginia and Maryland* (London, 1656).

7. Peter Wilson Coldham, *The Bristol Registers of Servants Sent to Foreign Plantations 1654-1686* (Baltimore, 1988). See also J. W. Wyatt, "Transportation from Gloucestershire, 1718-1773," *Gloucestershire Historical Studies*, Vol. 3 (1969), pp. 2-16.

8. *Gentleman's Magazine*, Vol. 34 (1764), p. 261. According to more recent estimates, about one in four British emigrants to colonial America during the eighteenth century were convicts: see, for example, Kenneth Morgan, "English and American Attitudes Towards Convict Transportation 1718-1775, *History*, Vol. 72 (1987), p.416.

9. James Boswell, *Life of Samuel Johnson* (London: Everyman's Library, 1949), Vol. 2, p. 312.

10. William Blackstone, *Commentaries on the Laws of England* (Oxford, 1765-9), Vol. 1, p. 137.

CHAPTER I

The Convicts and Their Background

Of the total number of convicts despatched to the Americas between 1614 and 1775, amounting to some 50,000 men, women and children, all but an insignificant minority belonged to the poorest class and most were sentenced for crimes which today might incur a small fine or, more likely, probation. Roughly half of all those sold into an American slavery were sentenced by the courts in and around London which, throughout its history, has acted as a magnet to the poor, the idle, the shiftless and the ambitious. To these we might add the honest adventurers who were drawn to London because its streets were, by legend, paved with gold. But the promise was false: regular work at a living wage was hard to come by and such charity as was dispensed was available only to those who could claim London as their birthplace. Within this populous city jobs were obtainable only through membership of one of the livery companies, and this had either to be paid for or attained after a long apprenticeship — both well beyond the resources of a migrant from out of town. Furthermore, unless a man could prove to the satisfaction of the local justices that he could maintain himself and his family from his own purse, or that he was a native of the parish in which he currently resided, he would be at severe risk of being forcibly moved on. The "parish cart" was a familiar part of the English landscape until late in the eighteenth century. It trundled from parish to parish depositing back in their supposed birthplaces those luckless individuals and families who had thought to make a new start elsewhere. For many parish overseers it must have seemed a relentless struggle, for no sooner was one cartload of illicit immigrants disposed of than a greater number would take their place, many of whom were bound to become either a prey to vice or a further burden on the ratepayers, or both, as indeed was acknowledged by contemporary observers:

7

Our Sessions Papers of late are crowded with instances of servant
maids robbing their Places . . . but all the while they make so
little reserve that, if they fall sick, the Parish must keep 'em; if
they are out of Place, they must Prostitute their Bodies or starve;
so that from chopping and changing they generally proceed to
whoring and thieving, and this is the reason why our Streets
swarm with Strumpets.[1]

Indicative of the attitude of parish officials of this time are the
official records relating to Daniel Newman and his wife Anne. In
January 1735 they and their family were evicted from the parish of
Clerkenwell in which they had taken up residence (thereby becoming
a charge on the poor rate) when it was discovered that they were
natives of Great Burstead in Essex. Once back in Burstead, Daniel
Newman took to crime to support himself and his family, for which
he was sentenced in November 1739 to be transported. After his
committal, Anne Newman found it impossible to provide for herself
and her two children and, being then far on in another pregnancy,
applied to the parish overseers for relief. For a few days Burstead
Parish supported her but then made an order for her and her family
to be moved back to Clerkenwell. But that parish "sought to bastardize
the two children [then aged four and two] and appealed at Essex
Quarter Sessions for a repeal of the order, pretending that Daniel
Newman had a former wife still living." Nevertheless the removal
order was confirmed and the little family was deposited back in
Clerkenwell. Remaining dissatisfied with this decision, Clerkenwell
"did again endeavour to get rid of the said two children . . . and,
on the oath of their mother (whom they now pretend to call Ann
Stafford) before the Middlesex Justices, they were prevailed upon to
order the removal of the children to Great Burstead." Yet another
appeal was made by Burstead Parish who were successful not only
in being awarded their legal costs but in having the Newmans removed
once more to Clerkenwell.[2]

Poor relief, such as it was, was meted out only to established
parishioners, and both parish and county records give abundant
evidence of the rigour and frequency with which suspected interlopers
were examined, and those without adequate proofs of birth or
residence remorselessly evicted via the parish cart. To survive at all
in the cities, where most of the money was, could mean taking what
casual labour was available at starvation wages and, for the rest,
living by one's wits. The temptation to take an easier road by making

a career on the wrong side of the law must have been irresistible to many; for some this would be but a convenient way to a life of relative ease, but for those whose families were threatened with starvation, the choice could be said to have been thrust upon them.

If poor environment encouraged the growth of vice, the condition of English cities in the seventeenth and eighteenth centuries must bear a heavy responsibility for the spectacular growth in crime in that time. The conditions in which the poor were housed almost defies description. Before the Great Plague of 1665 removed 100,000 of its citizens and the Great Fire a year later cleared many of its slums, London was a place where the stench from foul streams like the Fleet competed with the layers of refuse thrown out from overhanging houses and tenements; where filthy courts and blind alleys were impenetrable to light and air; and where night-soil was piled high against the city walls. During the summer months,

> flies pestered the houses in such multitudes that they lined the walls, and where thread or string hung down, it was presently thick-set with flies, like a rope of onions. Ants covered the highways, swarming so thickly that a handful at a time might be taken up, and the croaking of numerous frogs was loudly heard even before the ditches sheltering them could be seen.[3]

The metropolis of empire is elsewhere described as

> that many-gabled convivial old city [which] must have been a stronghold of stinks and unwholesomeness. No wonder that pestilence lingered in it. From time immemorial, successive generations of inhabitants, densely gathered there, had more and more befouled the ground . . . where the surface incorporated every excrement and refuse, and where the dead had their burial pits among the living. It had no wide streets for the wind to blow through. In general it had only alleys rather than streets: narrow, irregular passages, wherein houses of opposite sides often nearly met above the darkened fetid gangway. The houses themselves, mostly constructed of wood and plaster, had hereditary accumulations of ordure in vaults beneath them. Unsunned, unventilated dwellings, from when they were built, had been saturating themselves with steams of uncleanliness, and their walls and furniture must have stored an infinity of ancestral frowsiness and infection.[4]

After the Great Fire, many of the middle class were able to move to new and more sanitary quarters, but the poor were doomed to be huddled even more closely together in the old and newly-created slum dwellings. By the middle of the eighteenth century the City of London still had no drainage, and piles of rotting refuse, on which pigs browsed freely, lay everywhere. One of the larger midden heaps which adorned Grays Inn Lane was not removed until the beginning of the nineteenth century, following its sale to Russia for the manufacture of bricks. Household rubbish was customarily thrown into the streets, sheds and stalls were propped up against houses wherever room could be found for them, bullocks and mad dogs roamed loose in the streets, and swarms of beggars, thieves and prostitutes plied their trade unhindered, many after dark when the absence of street lighting was a distinct advantage to them. Other English cities rivalled London in squalor, each with its ghetto where the destitute poor rubbed shoulders with the petty criminal.

In the towns and countryside, though the physical environment may have been less oppressive, the labourer and hired hand shared with their city cousins the same economic misery. Average earnings by the end of the seventeenth century were stated by one authority[5] to have been: for a nobleman £3,200 a year, for a country gentleman £280, for a merchant £200-£400, for a farmer £42.10s., and for an artisan £30. A labourer engaged in husbandry or industry could earn at best one shilling a day, or not more than £18 a year. The poorest classes, including vagrants, thieves and beggars, were reckoned by the same authority to have had an average yearly income of £5, well below subsistence level. In the next century

> the agricultural labourer was further mulcted by enclosures . . . The Poor Law professed to find him work but was so administered that the reduction of his wages to a bare subsistence became an easy process and an economical expedient . . . His employers, who fixed his wages by their own authority, relieved their own estates at the expense of his poor luxuries . . . tied him to the soil and starved him by a prohibitive corn law . . . The freedom of the few was bought by the servitude of the many . . . No thought was given to their condition by the Legislature, unless it be that the attempt to repress by atrocious penal laws the violence which their unparalleled sufferings drove them occasionally to commit may be called thought.[6]

Authoritative voices were even found to justify this oppression. Andrew Fletcher of Saltoun, a Member of Parliament, went so far as to suggest that hopeless slavery was the proper condition for labourers, arguing that such people existed only to work and that politicians should be able to limit their existence by work.

As inescapable poverty led to an increase in crime, so began a spiral in which more and more punitive legislation was prescribed to counter the perceived problems. By 1770 the number of capital offences on the statute book was estimated in Parliament to have grown to 154 and, as might have been expected from such an accretion of extemporised laws, the code had become extravagant in its absurdities. The death penalty was prescribed for such varied felonies as: stealing a sheep or horse; snatching a man's property from his hands and running away with it; stealing an amount of forty shillings in a dwelling-house or to the amount of five shillings privately in a shop; picking a pocket of more than twelve pence; stealing linen from a bleaching ground or woollen cloth from a tenter ground; cutting down trees in a garden or orchard; or breaking the bounds of a fish-pond so that the fish escaped. But it was not a capital offence to make an attempt on the life of one's father; to commit premeditated perjury; to stab a man, provided that he did not die; or to burn down a house in which the arsonist had a lease, even though the lives of hundreds might be endangered. Death was the prescribed punishment for stealing goods to the value of forty shillings from a vessel on a navigable river but not for stealing the same amount from a vessel on a canal. To steal fruit which had already been picked was a felony, but to steal it by picking it was merely a trespass. To break a pane of glass at five in the afternoon in order to steal was a capital offence, but to break into a house violently at four o'clock on a summer's morning was merely a misdemeanour. A thief stealing goods from a shop, if he had the fortune to be seen, was subject to transportation, but if he passed unobserved, he merited the death penalty. A servant who was put on trial for having attempted to kill his master by striking him fifteen times with a hatchet was executed, not for attempted murder, but as a burglar because he had been obliged to lift the latch on his master's door in order to enter his chamber.[7]

It was to the advantage of the professional criminal to be at least as well acquainted with the intricacies of penal law as were the justices who dispensed it and, for their mutual protection, to inhabit the same parts of each city even when they did not operate in a gang. Inevitably the poorest class were driven to the same already overcrowded tenements in the cities where petty crime, prostitution and beggary were a way of life, and from there it was an easy graduation into organised crime, which alone might appear to offer the promise of regular and substantial reward coupled with at least some comradely protection against the full rigour of the draconian laws. When the worst happened and a professional was caught, he was often able to shrug off the direst consequences. The confraternity was well versed in procuring alibis and false witnesses and, even when these did not work and a sentence of transportation followed, money could still buy privilege. Thus the proceeds of crime could buy a private cabin for the voyage to America, instant freedom on arrival and, if desired, a quick return passage to England — though this last was a recourse only for the intrepid, since the penalty for returning from transportation before the expiry of the term of sentence was death by hanging.

In October 1728 the King wrote to the justices of the City of London to express his concern at "the frequent robberies of late committed in the streets of London, Westminster and parts adjacent . . . which are greatly to be imputed to the unlawful return of felons who have been transported to our Plantations." He ordered a reward of £40 (a huge sum for the time) to be paid to any person "who shall discover any of them so as they may be apprehended and brought to justice . . . and condign punishment [i.e. death]." This measure was reinforced in 1743 by "An Act for the more Easy and Effectual Conviction of Offenders Found at Large after being Ordered for Transportation."

Organised crime and gang violence reached unprecedented heights in the cities in the first quarter of the eighteenth century. Even the young bloods from the upper classes now made their contribution towards terrorising the London streets by joining vicious groups such as the Mowhawks or the Hell Fire Club, and conspiracies, arson, highway robbery and impudent thefts were everywhere reported. The City Marshal of London was quoted as saying that in 1712 he had personally known 2,000 people in the city to live entirely by thieving but that, by the 1720s, the number of professional thieves had risen to almost 12,000. Crime on this scale demanded professional organisation and the services of those whose talent lay more in planning and organising crime than in its execution. The need produced a new class of super-criminal bearing more than a passing resemblance to latter-day Mafia godfathers. The malign genius of the contemporary London underworld was undoubtedly Jonathan Wild, whose long, successful, but ultimately fatal career began when he was an inmate of a debtors' prison. By 1710, and with an effrontery which characterised all his activities, he had opened an agency where those who had lost (in his own euphemistic term) any of their possessions could buy them back. This agency was impudently styled "The Office for the Recovery of Lost and Stolen Property":

> As soon as any thing is missing, reported to be stolen, the first course we steer is directly to the office of Mr. Jonathan Wild . . . We are looked up to as good chaps and welcome to redeem it. But this was in the infancy of the establishment. Now they are grown wiser and calculate exactly what silver and gold will melt down for.[8]

To this secure income the State added regular supplements, happy to recompense Wild for hunting and apprehending those criminals who were not of his own confraternity, and for breaking up those gangs who set up in rivalry. His success in such ventures earned him the title of "Thief Taker Extraordinary." While parish constables had jurisdiction only within their own parishes, Wild's men could move freely all over the country, and he appointed agents in the principal ports and county towns whose duties were to report on all criminal activities, including their own. Lured by the huge rewards offered for the apprehension of convicts who returned to England before the expiry of their sentences of transportation, Wild found it expedient to enter into a close and apparently cordial relationship with the then transportation contractor, Jonathan Forward, whose intelligence in these matters was unrivalled. Felons returning too early from transportation were an excellent source of income: if they could not be blackmailed into an extended life of crime or for hush money, the State stood always ready to pay the statutory £40 for their betrayal. As his profits grew, Wild was able to employ a ship of his own to export stolen goods to Holland which he sold for contraband, including spirits and condoms, to be freighted back to England.

But Wild finally overreached himself and was brought to justice in May 1725 to become the year's most celebrated victim of the gallows. Before his trial, he distributed amongst the jurymen and others a great number of printed papers headed, "A List of persons discovered, apprehended and convicted of several robberies upon the

Highway; and also for Burglary and House-Breaking; and also for returning from Transportation: by Jonathan Wild."[9] Though Wild's was the best organised and most notorious of the rookeries of the time, it was far from being the only such establishment. Fagin's kitchens abounded in the more squalid parts of London, not only providing a haven and protective association for their members, but developing crime as a serious full-time profession. Training for the craft began in infancy and child-felons were instructed how to safeguard their own interests and those of their particular association. Sarah Bibby was one such, a member of a thieves' den presided over by Harry White of St. Bride's Parish who specialised in recruiting waifs and strays to the profession. Sarah was "trained up to felony from her cradle" and was no more than thirteen years of age when, in April 1745, she gave evidence against Jack Price, a lad one year younger than herself, and succeeded in having him sentenced for stealing razors in Smithfield. She boasted openly to her rivals in crime that "she had hanged five or six last Sessions and would hang many more." Elizabeth Stavenaugh, also brought to court on Sarah's evidence, testified: "My child has gone a thieving with her and is transported." Sarah's career, in England at least, was short-lived for in December 1745 she was herself apprehended and sentenced to transportation.[10]

Another professional villain, John Courtney, flourished at about the same time. One of his former associates, Thomas Welch, while awaiting execution at Newgate for highway robbery, made a statement accusing Courtney of being

> a most notorious, wicked man who has been guilty of divers robberies and other atrocious offences . . . Many persons, upon Courtney's evidence only, have suffered the death penalty for the sake of the reward . . . One of his wives was last execution day executed for returning from transportation who, about a year ago, the said Courtney by force rescued out of the prison in order to avoid the just punishment she deserved. Now Courtney cohabits with a most infamous pickpocket who goes by the name of Black Moll by whom he is supported by means of her iniquitous practices.[11]

The majority of those transported to the colonies may, however, be justly regarded as having fallen victim to oppressive circumstances and harsh environment rather than as professional villains. In recognition of this, the more humane justices and court officials frequently exercised what clemency they could within the confines of a rigid penal code. There is good reason to believe, for example, that the value of goods stolen was often assessed at well below any realistic appraisal so as to avoid the imposition of an automatic death penalty; and the fact that so many were transported for the crime of stealing a handkerchief lends weight to the suspicion that this was accepted as a "token" indictment both by the prosecution and defence in substitution for a capital offence. Even after sentence had been passed, a felon, his wife, relatives, neighbours or influential friends were free to appeal to the King for a pardon. On the one hand it is remarkable how few of such petitions were made relative to the large numbers sentenced and, on the other, how many seemed to succeed against the odds because of a perceived need to mitigate the general harshness of the law's exactions.

At a lower level in the social scale, but still part of the legal establishment, were those such as the parish constables and watchmen who, even when unbribed, were often known to turn a blind eye where there was a humanitarian or practical incentive. Despite the rigorous penalties prescribed by the law against those returning from transportation before the expiry of their terms, and the handsome rewards paid to prosecutors who succeeded in securing a conviction under this head, the courts experienced great difficulties both in proving identity and establishing the fact of previous transportation. It was probably for those reasons that the London watchman who arrested John Law in 1772 was led to answer in court: "I have seen him several times in Smithfield since he returned from transportation and have begged him to get out of the way for fear I should have charge of him."[12] Law, who had been despatched to America by the *Douglas* in 1769, was able to secure a pardon for his offence in January 1773.

Once the legal process had been set in motion however, little account appears to have been taken of personal circumstances. Evidence from Sessions records suggests that, as an integral part of the punishment of transportation, care was often taken to send members of the same family who were sentenced together to different colonies by different ships. Husbands and wives of those transported to the colonies were, of course, free to book their passage on the same ship as their partners if they could afford it, or to indenture themselves for service in the same colony if they could not, but very

few took this course. There is a sad story on record of Elizabeth
Martin, arrested in 1766 for stealing a silver spoon. While sharing a
drink with a companion in a local hostelry she had enquired how to
go about securing her transportation, for she longed to join her
husband who had already been "cast for the colonies" at the Maidstone
Assizes (probably Jonathan Martin sentenced in 1764). A bystander
had suggested ironically that she should visit a nearby goldsmith's
shop — and less than a week later she was charged at the Old Bailey
for stealing a spoon from a tavern in Kingham Street. While confined
in Newgate awaiting trial, she confided her desire to be transported
to one of the maidservants who laughed at what she thought was a
joke. When her case came up before the Recorder of London and
she offered no defence beyond her wish to be reunited with her
husband, he explained that, if she was transported, "perhaps you may
not go to the same colony or be disposed of in some other part of
the country, [and] you may never see each other." Perversely Elizabeth
Martin was fined ten pence for her offence and whipped.[13]

Once a felon had been detained in prison and then shipped off to
the colonies, his wife and family were most often left to fend for
themselves as best they could, in the last resort becoming participants
in crime themselves or, perhaps worse, committed to drudgery in a
parish workhouse where the diseased, beggars, vagrants, lunatics,
prostitutes and the honest poor were herded together under the same
roof. The life expectancy of a child taken into a workhouse was
short. A House of Commons report of 1767 discloses that, out of
every 100 children born in London workhouses in 1763, or received
there while under the age of twelve months, only seven survived
until 1765. Those workhouse children who managed to cling to life
were often hired out to local contractors to defray the cost of
maintaining them. Following the 1767 report, Parliament enacted that
babies and young children should be sent into the care of foster
mothers who lived at least five miles from the capital, a piece of
legislation known sardonically amongst the poor as "The Act for
Keeping Children Alive." From this date there were 2,000 fewer
burials each year in London,[14] but the wholesale deportation of infants
to new factories in the North seems merely to have transferred the
problem. John Fielden, Member of Parliament for Oldham and himself
a manufacturer, provided ample evidence that thousands of children
from the age of seven were sent into the factories to be worked to
the utmost by cruel overseers; many were harried, beaten and starved
to the point of death, and a few even committed suicide.[15]

The prevailing dread in English parishes of acquiring any additions to the poor rate extended as much to broken families as to those without work, and it was much to their advantage to encourage the flow of emigrants. The Mayor of Bristol reported:

> Among those who repair to Bristol from all parts to be transported for servants to His Majesty's plantations beyond seas, some are husbands that have forsaken their wives, others wives who have abandoned their husbands; some are children and apprentices run away from their parents and masters; oftentimes unwary and credulous persons have been tempted on board by men-stealers, and many that have been pursued by hue-and-cry for robberies, burglaries or breaking prison, do thereby escape the prosecution of laws and justice.[16]

NOTES

1. Andrew Moreton, *Every Body's Business* (London, 1725), pp. 6-7.

2. Greater London Record Office: Middlesex Sessions Book No. 968, pp. 38-43.

3. Walter G. Bell, *The Great Plague in London* (London, 1924), pp. 15, 94.

4. Sir John Simon, *English Sanitary Institutions* (London, 1890), p. 101.

5. Gregory King, *Natural and Political Observations and Conclusions upon the State and Condition of England* (London, 1696, reprinted Baltimore, 1936).

6. James E. T. Rogers, *Six Centuries of Work and Wages* (London, 1884), pp. 488-489.

7. Quoted from E. H. Lecky, *A History of England in the Eighteenth Century* (London, 1920), Vol. 7, pp. 316-317.

8. Bernard de Mandeville, *Enquiry into the Causes of the Frequent Executions at Tyburn* (London, 1725).

9. *Newgate Calendar*, ed. Sir Norman Birkett (London, 1951), pp. 104-105.

10. Old Bailey Sessions Papers for December 1745.

11. Petition of Thomas Welch in PRO (Public Record Office): State Papers SP 36/149. Black Moll, *alias* Mary Baxter, *alias* Mary Jones, was condemned for theft at Exeter in 1753 and reprieved to be transported for fourteen years. In 1757 she was discovered at large in London and narrowly escaped the death penalty. She was transported for life to Maryland by the *Tryal* in September 1758.

12. Old Bailey Sessions Papers for December 1772.

13. Old Bailey Sessions Papers for September 1766.

14. See J. Howlett, *Examination of Dr. Price's Essay on the Population of England and Wales* (Maidstone, 1781).

15. John Fielden, *The Curse of the Factory System* (London, 1836), pp. 5-6.

16. *Calendar of State Papers, Colonial Series, 1661-1668* (London, 1880), No. 311, p. 98.

CHAPTER II

The Prisons

By the middle of the eighteenth century Henry Fielding was able to comment that "there are few, if any, nations or countries where the poor . . . are in a more scandalous, nasty condition than here in England."[1] The abundance of the poor and of draconian laws to protect property combined to ensure that prison populations were maintained at a high level. William Blackstone estimated that in his time there were 160 offences meriting the death penalty,[2] and this number was to be increased substantially in ensuing years.

London alone boasted fourteen prisons of which the most ancient and notorious was Newgate. Dick Whittington, three times Lord Mayor of London between 1397 and 1420, bequeathed money for its repair and, in commemoration of his gift, his cat was carved upon the outer gate. Through this gate some 20,000 felons passed on the first step of their long journey to America. In 1754 it was described as

> a large prison and made very strong the better to secure such sort of criminals which too much fill it. It is a dismal place within. The prisoners are sometimes packed so close together, and the air so corrupted by their stench and nastiness, that it occasions a disease called the Jail Distemper of which they die by dozens, and cartloads of them are carried out and thrown into a pit in the churchyard of Christchurch without ceremony; and so infectious is this distemper that several judges, jurymen and lawyers etc. have taken it off the prisoners when they have been brought to the Old Bailey to be tried, and died soon after . . . And to this wretched place innocent people are sometimes sent, and loaded with irons before their trial, not to secure them but to extort money from them by a merciless jailor; for if they have money to bribe him they may have the irons as light as they

please . . . Sweet herbs are strewed in the court and passages of it to prevent infection; and the snuffing up of vinegar, it is said, is the most likely way to preserve the healths of those that are obliged to attend . . . trials.[3]

To Londoners Newgate was known, with reason, as "hell above ground." Fees were extorted by the jailers for almost every service, and it went hard with those unable or unwilling to pay. If prisoners required bedding it could be hired from the turnkey, otherwise they shared the filthy straw strewn over the stone floor. Other London prisons imposed similar exactions. One inmate of the Fleet who was confined for debt in 1729 and who refused to pay his fees "had irons put upon his legs, which were too little, so that in putting them on his legs were like to have been broken. He was dragged away into the dungeon, where he lay without a bed, and loaded with irons so close rivetted that they kept him in continual torment and mortified his legs."[4] In the following year the prison chaplain reported that he had visited an inmate whose legs and feet were so swollen from his irons and from the great cold that he was unable to rise, and died a few days later.

After arrest by the parish constable, a suspect would be carted to the "hold" at Newgate where all prisoners, convicted or awaiting trial, were kept. This room, dark and with a floor of stone, was entered by a hatch measuring fifteen by twenty feet. Inside the "hold" was one wooden barrack bed on which, according to a description given in 1707, "you may repose yourself if your nose suffer you to rest." Around the room were ring bolts to which prisoners considered to be disorderly were chained. The fee for securing removal from here to more salubrious quarters was two shillings and six pence. As soon as prisoners entered the jail, heavy iron manacles were clapped on their hands and feet unless they were prepared to buy "easement" from the turnkey.

To add to their own physical and mental sufferings, Newgate prisoners could scarcely avoid witnessing the even grosser brutalities inflicted on others. From here women were dragged away to be burned alive for murdering their husbands or, until as late as 1753, for clipping coins. For this same offence of coin-clipping, the sentence for men, until 1670, was hanging, drawing and quartering, after which their remains, including their heads, were boiled and salted in that part of the prison known as Jack Ketch's Kitchen.

Thomas Ellwood, a Quaker friend of Milton and Penn, who was thrown into Newgate in 1662 for attending a Friends' service, described the prison as hell on earth, being a large and round prison, having in the middle a stout oak pillar which held up the chapel above. At night the prisoners there fastened their hammocks at one end to this pillar and, at the other, to the wall in three tiers up to the ceiling until there was no further space. Then on the stone floor a fourth layer was stretched out with rough beds being provided for the sick and weakly.

> When we first came into Newgate there lay in a little place like a closet in the room where we were lodged, the quartered bodies of three men who had been executed some days before for a real or pretended plot, and the reason why their quarters lay there so long was that the relatives were all that while petitioning to have leave to bury them; which at length, with much ado, was obtained for the quarters but not for the heads, which were ordered to be set up in some part of the City. I saw the heads when they were brought up to be boiled; the hangman fetched them in a dirty dust basket out of some by-place, and setting them down among the felons, he and they made great sport with them. They took them by the hair, flouting, jeering, and laughing at them; and then, giving them ill-names, boxed them on the ears and cheeks. Which done, the Hangman put them into his Kettle and parboiled them with Bay-salt and Cummin-seed — that to keep them from putrefaction and this to keep off the fowls from seizing on them. The whole sight . . . was both frightful and loathsome and begat an abhorrence in my nature.[5]

As the law then stood, a person convicted of theft was liable to forfeit his possessions to the Crown, so that some courageous spirits, accused of this offence, refused to plead in order to protect their families. Until this law was amended in 1714, such foolhardiness could be punished by *peine forte et dure*: offenders were taken to Newgate where their bodies were stretched by ropes while large stones and heavy weights were laid upon their bodies thus slowly crushing all life out of them unless or until they changed their minds. Even after this barbaric means of persuasion was overtaken by more humane legislation, prisoners who refused to plead could still be coaxed to another view on application of a whipcord thumbscrew.

Outside the walls of Newgate condemned prisoners were regularly and ceremoniously hanged with the intention of deterring crime. These ritual executions, which Horace Walpole described as England's favourite amusement, rivalled the theatre in attracting large crowds. Up to 20,000 people at a time would assemble for the spectacle and tickets for viewing space, particularly in a nearby tavern, were keenly sought after. Those with a taste for it could also divert themselves by observing the antics of the inmates of the madhouses, attend public whippings or, after 1752, become spectators at Surgeons' Hall to study the method of dissection of executed murderers. Public whipping, either at a post or at the tail of a cart, was a regular feature of life for minor offenders. Physical punishment was such a familiar and routine part of penal correction that every prison turnkey would arm himself and his favourites with "a flexible weapon."

Women taken into Newgate might find themselves more leniently treated in anticipation of their services. A very large room on the top floor of the prison was used for

> those that lie for transportation, and they, knowing their time to be short here, rather than bestow one minute towards cleaning the same, suffer themselves to lie far worse than swine . . . for they are almost poisoned by their own filth, and their conversation is nothing but one continued course of swearing, cursing and debauchery . . . Women in every ward of this prison are exceedingly worse than the worst of men, not only in respect of nastiness and indecency of living, but more especially as to their conversation which . . . is so profane and wicked as hell itself can be.[6]

A seventeenth-century account of Newgate speaks more plainly: "Gatekeepers and petty officers of the prison consider all women prisoners of their seraglio and indulge themselves in the promiscuous use of as many of them as they please."[7] While nearly a hundred years later:

> The men and women prisoners are all put together till they are locked up at night, and have perpetual opportunities of retiring to the dark cells as much as they please; the women indeed are such as do not need much solicitation in this commerce . . . As many of them are totally destitute of both money and friends, they would have no alternative but to become prostitutes or perish with hunger.[8]

Women prisoners posed other problems too. The Keeper of Newgate, ordered to report on his difficulties in excluding spirits from the prison (at a time when the King's Bench Prison ran thirty gin shops selling 120 gallons each week) found that "women, who are chiefly the conveyors of them, secrete them in such ways that it would be termed the grossest insult to search for them."

In the Bridewell, a prison set aside to receive errant women, "all strumpets, night walkers, pickpockets, vagrant and idle persons that are taken up for their ill tricks, as also incorrigible and disobedient servants . . . are forced to beat hemp in public view with due correction of whipping." Hogarth's drawing of the place shows one wretch hanging from a pillory by her wrists under a placard reading "Better to work than to stand thus," and on the whipping post another inscription: "The reward of idleness." The Bridewell was one of the more popular venues for those wishing to be edified by the sight of public whipping which was carried out on all alike, including women and children, by stripping them to the waist and applying the whip according to the formulary "until the body should be bloody."[9] Not until 1817 was the practice of whipping women in public abolished in England.

When women were arraigned on capital charges, they would often attempt to escape the death penalty by pleading that they were pregnant, and indeed many achieved this condition after their imprisonment. The law was merciful enough to defer execution until after the child was born, but then the mother was "called down to her previous judgment," often commuted to a period of transportation. Children born in this way were given into the care, first of the prison nurses, and then to the overseers of the poor. The number of women who "pleaded their bellies" was so numerous, and their plea so often desperately false, that each was taken for examination before a Panel of Matrons who would report back to the court on their findings. No record survives to inform us what qualifications, if any, the matrons possessed, nor what methods they used in an age of prevailing medical ignorance to carry out their task. In 1804, when this system still survived, a woman named Anne Hurle "contrived to baffle the skill of the women appointed to examine her" to the extent that they could come to no satisfactory decision. A doctor was called in, Anne Hurle was declared not pregnant, and was soon hanged.

Moll Flanders tells how her mother successfully "pleaded her belly" and, when she was transported after giving birth, left Moll "about half a year old and in bad hands, you may be sure."[10] She was, perhaps, more fortunate than most in her plight, for separation of mother and child appears normally to have occurred much sooner. Sarah Bodington, a Newgate prisoner pardoned for transportation in 1680, made oath that

> for the space of three months next before the tyme of her being brought to the Gaole, she dwelt and was legally settled in the house of Moses Lizado Barrows of St. James, Duke's Place, as a servant, and was begott with child by him; whereuppon it is ordered by this Courte that Wm. Boddington, an infant about nyne weeks old, be sent and left with the Churchwardens and Overseers of the Poore of the said parish . . . to be kept & provided for and mainteyned untill they can discharge themselves by due course of Lawe.[11]

Medical science not only served the law but was well served by it. The courts supplied regular material for the dissection tables as well as living subjects for experiment. Convicted felons were much in demand for medical experiments such as that conducted in 1721 on six Newgate prisoners — three men and three women — awaiting transportation who received a free pardon after consenting to inoculation against smallpox, "an experiment frequently practised in foreign parts and made even here."[12] No doubt hoping to benefit under a similar dispensation, though at apparently greater personal cost, Charles Ray, also in Newgate in the same year, offered to allow the doctors to remove his ear drum for experimentation, if he could be pardoned transportation.[13] George Chippendale, sentenced to hang in 1763 for robbery with violence, was reprived on the eve of his execution on condition that he submitted to the amputation of a quite healthy limb. The sole purpose of the operation was to test the efficacy of a newly-invented styptic which was claimed to be less painful than the existing method. Chippendale, according to the official record, accepted this offer thankfully, but the College of Surgeons, while accepting that the styptic was effective in the treatment of animals, ventured the opinion that experimentation on a human being was often "fallacious and inconclusive."[14] In the event, Chippendale was pardoned for his original offence and transported for life in July 1763.

More reluctant beneficiaries from the ample supply of pardoned convicts were the Army and Royal Navy, especially in times of war when both ships and men were pressed into State service. Between 1702 and 1714, when Marlborough was ranging through Europe, from

1743 to 1748 during King George's War, and again from 1755 to 1763 during the French and Indian Wars, a felon awaiting execution or transportation stood an excellent chance of receiving a royal pardon if he "volunteered" for naval or military service. The Navy's view of such arrangements was expressed in 1771:

> Such persons may not only bring distempers and immoralities among their companions but may discourage men of irreproachable characters from entering His Majesty's service, seeing they are to be ranked with common malefactors.[15]

But as Dr. Samuel Johnson observed: "No man will be a sailor who has contrivance enough to get himself into a gaol, for being in a ship is being in gaol, with the chance of being drowned."

Economic considerations dictated not only recruitment to the armed forces but the regulation of penal institutions, and private enterprise played its part here just as much as in mercantile affairs. In the towns and countryside nearly as many prisons were in private hands as were maintained by the local authorities, and these were required to pay their owners a return on their investment. Few were buildings originally designed for this use, and old dungeons and gatehouses were pressed into service. Where walls were at risk of tumbling down from neglect and prisoners likely to escape, it was cheaper to load them with irons than to make repairs. Private owners would frequently farm-let their prisons to local tenants who then recouped the rent by extorting excessive sums from the inmates for food and for easing the more brutal punishments. A charge was even levied for "turning the key" when a prisoner was released. The town prison of Chesterfield, Derbyshire, owned by the Duke of Portland, consisted of one room with a cellar underneath for which the Keeper paid an annual rent of fifteen guineas. The jail in Ely, Cambridgeshire, was the property of the Bishop of Ely, and was so decrepit that the Keeper felt obliged "to chain [prisoners] down across their backs upon a floor across which were several iron bars, with an iron collar with spikes about their necks, and a heavy iron bar across their legs." [16]

An account of fees taken by the Keeper of Newgate in 1745 included the following:[17]

For every debtor's discharge	8s.10d.
For every felon's discharge	18s.10d.
For every misdemeanour	14s.10d.

For every felon's entrance on the Master's Side	10s. 6d.
For every person admitted to the Press Yard	£3. 3s. 0d.
For every transport's discharge	14s.10d.

The appointment as Keeper of Newgate appears to have been no sinecure, complained against both by the prisoners for his oppressive discipline and grasping exactions and by the parsimonious justices for his liberality and tolerance of disorder. He was expected to cope, moreover, with persistent overcrowding which arose in great part from the frequent failure of the transportation contractors to find enough ships to clear the prison. By November 1735 there were 139 convicts from five previous sessions at the Old Bailey lying in Newgate awaiting ships to transport them. Such was the crush that additional rooms in that dismal building had to be adapted to accommodate them all. Jonathan Forward was summoned to answer before the Lord Mayor of London for his apparent slackness and, in spite of his plea that ships were lacking, was browbeaten into an agreement that he would in future clear Newgate Jail of those "cast for transportation" three times a year, in March, August and December. The problem, however, persisted for several years more. Forward was again arraigned for the same reason in the following year and, in 1749, his successor, Andrew Reid, was accused of the same dereliction and pleaded the same excuse.[18] On 26 March 1751 the Secretary to the Treasury intervened to complain to the Lord Mayor that Reid's contract was being evaded and to insist that it should be more rigidly enforced than in the past in order to prevent the great increase in robberies that had taken place. The Treasury also now demanded that the captains of transport ships should enter into a financial bond to procure certificates of the landing of convicts at colonial ports.[19] The fact that no landing certificates later in date than 1736 are to be found in the Corporation of London records suggests that the relevant provision in the Transportation Act of 1718 had long since been consigned to oblivion, nor does the Treasury's new-found concern on the point appear to have been translated into action. By 1752 the situation had deteriorated to such a point that James Armour, Reid's agent, was ordered to pay £14.17s.6d. to recompense the city for the additional charges which it had incurred by continuing to house felons beyond the time when they should have taken ship.[20] Not until 1760, when the City of London proposed a petition be made to the King for him to order sentences of transportation to be put into immediate execution,[21] and the appointment shortly thereafter of a more efficient contractor, John Stewart, did the transportation scheme finally settle to its intended rhythm.

The appalling and insanitary conditions prevailing within Newgate merely accentuated the internal strife which was, even in better times, always to be expected from prisoners who were half-starved, ill clothed, and had only the gloomiest expectations. Some found ingenious solutions to their worst problems: in 1712 a great number of the inmates were discovered to be attending divine service, not out of any sudden access of piety, but "passing through the Chapel . . . where some prisoners and their servants eat and drink off the Communion Table." An order was made for those prisoners who did not attend the service with the right dispositions to be locked up while it went on.[22]

Far more prisoners died from hunger, deprivation and disease in English prisons than ever went to the gallows, and Blackstone described the jailers of his day as "a merciless race of men, and being conversant with scenes of misery, steeled against any tender sensation." In Newgate and other jails, poor inmates were allowed to beg for food and other necessities from charitably inclined passers-by in order to supplement the poor rations allowed them. Wherever they went, the male prisoners were shackled in irons and, when called to trial, could be required to walk from ten to fifteen miles chained together.[23] After the Scottish rebellion of 1745, several hundred prisoners were brought to Liverpool to be shipped off to the plantations. Over 400 were taken by barges to the waiting ships but, when one overturned, eight were drowned because they were handcuffed.[24] In June 1764 fifty-six men and thirteen women from Newgate were put aboard a lighter to join a transport ship (the *Dolphin*) at Blackwall, and it was recorded that only the men were chained and that thirteen of the convicts who were ill were permitted to travel by coaches.[25]

Though the law could and did demand the most terrible retribution, the power of money was always able to mitigate its worst exactions. Rarely was a gentleman of any substance transported for a criminal act, and even a notorious felon, with the aid of his ill-gotten gains, could purchase a comfortable passage to America and secure his immediate freedom on arrival. Daniel Crawford, "a Scotsman of fair complexion and small stature," was sentenced in Middlesex in February 1729 to be transported for seven years, was duly landed in Annapolis, Maryland in June of that year and promptly given his freedom on payment to the ship's captain of a bill of exchange for £10 drawn on John Govan of Basinghall Lane, London, merchant. Govan was acting on behalf of a man called Thomas Peter, in Glasgow, who in 1731 wrote a grudging letter of thanks to Govan ending: "I assure you I have no money to bestow for delivery of a rogue from the halter, nor never will give a sixpence that way for I have a large family of my own to provide for. He [Crawford], being a tradesman, I doubt not but he will be so grateful as to send you what you have been out for him."[26]

In 1736, while 100 felons were made to walk in chains from Newgate to Blackfriars to be packed on a lighter to take them to their ship (the *Patapsco Merchant*), five "gentlemen of distinction" named as [William] Wreathock, attorney, Henry Justice Esq., barrister-at-law, [George] Vaughan, [George] Bird and [William] Ruffhead, who had also been sentenced to transportation, rode to Blackwall in two hackney coaches "attended by Jonathan Forward Esq. . . . [and] were accommodated with the captain's cabin which they stored with plenty of provisions for their voyage and travels."[27]

Bribes, under whatever guise they masqueraded, bought relief from almost any of the grosser forms of punishment except the death penalty — but, even here, a gift to the executioner would guarantee swift and competent despatch. With the aid of money, branding could be carried out with a cool iron and a whipping accomplished without damage to a tender skin. "Burning in the hand," wrote Bentham, "according as the criminal and the executioner can agree, is performed either with a cold or a red-hot iron; and if it be a red-hot iron, it is only a slice of ham which is burnt; to complete the farce, the criminal screams whilst it is only the fat which smokes and burns; and the knowing spectators only laugh at this parody of justice."[28] But at times even the law's worst exactions seemed to lag behind public demand for retribution. A contributor to the *Gentleman's Magazine* in 1750 not only insisted on a return to branding on the cheek but suggested castration for male offenders and transportation for all convicted women at their very first offence, "be it greater or less."[29]

For the poor, of course, there was little easement to be found. For them the punishment to be feared above other physical cruelties was that of transportation, which Sir John Fielding, one of the more humane luminaries of the Middlesex Bench and himself responsible for many hundreds of such sentences, regarded as "the wisest and most humane punishment. For it immediately removes the evil, separates the individual from his abandoned connexions, and gives him a fresh opportunity of being a useful member of society."[30] Even Fielding had to concede, however, that those who had experienced one term of transportation would choose the death sentence in preference to a second term.

NOTES

1. *An Enquiry into the Causes of the Late Increase of Robbers* (London, 1751), sec. iv.

2. *Commentaries on the Laws of England*, 18th ed. (London, 1829), Vol. 4, p. 18.

3. Rosamond Bayne Powell, *Eighteenth Century London Life* (London, 1937), pp. 209-210.

4. Report on Conditions in the Fleet Prison in *House of Commons Journal* for 1729, p. 513.

5. *History of the Life of Thomas Ellwood*, ed. S. Graveson (London, 1906), pp. 14-15.

6. William Eden Hooper, *History of Newgate and the Old Bailey* (London, 1935), p. 26 ff., quoted from *A Description of Newgate* by "B.L." of Twickenham.

7. Anthony Babington, *The English Bastille* (London, 1971), p. 96.

8. *Gentleman's Magazine*, Vol. 27 (1757), p. 268.

9. E. G. O'Donoghue, *The Bridewell Hospital* (London, 1929), pp. 174-175.

10. Daniel Defoe, *Moll Flanders* (London: Mayflower Books, 1964), p.14.

11. CLRO (Corporation of London Record Office): Sessions Book (10 September 1680).

12. PRO (Public Record Office): State Papers Criminal, 44/80/434.

13. *Ibid.*, SP44/79a/434.

14. Old Bailey Sessions Papers for May 1763.

15. *Calendar of Home Office Papers 1770-1772* (London, 1881), No. 604, p. 228.

16.   Arthur Griffiths, *The Chronicles of Newgate* (London, 1987), p. 268.

17.   CLRO: Repertory 149, f.103.

18.   Repertory 141, ff. 270, 358; 153, f. 236.

19.   Repertory 155, f. 252.

20.   Repertory 156, f. 193.

21.   Repertory 165, f. 99.

22.   Repertory 117, f. 70.

23.   John Howard, *An Account of the Present State of Prisons* (London, 1789), p. 19.

24.   *Gentleman's Magazine*, Vol. 17 (1747), p. 246.

25.   *London Magazine* (June 1764).

26.   CLRO: Misc. MSS, 366.11.

27.   *Gentleman's Magazine*, Vol. 6 (1736), p. 290.

28.   Because a brand mark in the hand could be easily concealed, an Act of 1699 ordained that branding should be "in the most visible part of the cheek nearest the nose" but since this made it almost impossible for those so scarred to get work, the Act was repealed in 1706.

29.   Vol. 20, pp. 532-533.

30.   *Calendar of Home Office Papers*, ed. R. A. Roberts (London, 1899), Vol. 4, No. 39.

CHAPTER III

The Dispensers of Justice

At the lowest level, justice was dispensed in England through the Courts of Quarter Session held regularly in every county and borough and presided over by justices of the peace. These, usually members of the gentry with some knowledge of the law, were appointed by the Crown, usually without salary, not only to administer the King's justice within their jurisdictions but, in the words of Sir Edward Coke (1552-1634), "to provide a form of subordinate government for the tranquillity and quiet of the realm." The J.P., with the help of constables appointed by each parish, acted as the police authority and was empowered to confine, try and sentence minor offenders with or without the assistance of a jury. Those arrested on suspicion of having committed serious crimes he would commit to prison to await trial before the King's Judges of Assize. With or without the benefit of a jury trial, a prisoner of low degree would find the scales of justice weighed heavily against him. Before the Civil War in England, a prisoner was confined and was unable to prepare a defence or call witnesses on his own behalf. Even after 1660, when more equitable procedures were instituted, counsel was not permitted to address a jury on a prisoner's behalf, and it was not until well into the eighteenth century that tolerable defence practices were introduced.

Through the years many complaints were levelled against the justices for their slackness and incompetence, but it was not until the eighteenth century that their powers were so widely abused as to become a public scandal. The seeds of trouble were sown when the Government began to appoint justices of the peace who might be better relied upon to support the political faction in power, and the old type of civilised country gentleman was increasingly replaced in the towns and cities by party hacks of humbler origin. Middle class burghers newly appointed to the unsalaried magistracy were easy prey to the offer of inflated fees for the issue of warrants, summonses and other judicial orders. The Middlesex Bench, which dealt with one in three of all the criminal cases arising in England, became notorious for its inefficiency and corruption. Its justices were described by Edmund Burke as the scum of the earth. So adept were they at drumming up new business to line their own pockets that they soon earned the epithet of "trading" or "basket" judges. Some dispensed justice and groceries from the same shop, using touts to advertise their trade; others would grant warrants on credit in order to stimulate litigation. Bribes were accepted from publicans for licences and from brothel keepers for protection.

Despite the glaring weaknesses of the system, however, it still managed to produce justices as honest and humane as Henry Fielding,[1] who was appointed to the Westminster Bench in 1748 when he was a very poor man. His novels pillory ferociously the "Justices of Mean Degree" who relished their power to give prison sentences or to indulge in "a little stripping and whipping," especially if they could please the local gentry thereby. He scourged the London magistrates for their extortions, having succeeded a reasonably upright justice, Sir Thomas De Veil, who openly proclaimed that he made £1,000 a year from his fees.

John Fielding, the half-blind brother of Henry, succeeded him as Chief Magistrate at Bow Street, and during his long tenure of office, from 1754 to 1780, completely reformed the Westminster Bench, though in the country beyond many abuses continued unabated. Fielding wrote of himself:

> I had not plundered the public or the poor of those sums which men who are always ready to plunder both as much as they can have been pleased to suspect me of taking: on the contrary, by composing instead of inflaming the quarrels of porters and beggars (which I blush to say hath not been universally practised), and by refusing to take a shilling from a man who most undoubtedly would not have had another left, I had reduced an income of about £500 a year of the dirtiest money on earth to little more than £300.[2]

In contrast, Tobias Smollet paints a picture of a country justice who, though perhaps not typical, was frequently to be met with. His Justice Gobble, while up in London as a journeyman hosier, "had picked up some law terms by conversing with hackney writers and attorneys' clerks of the lowest order," and secured his appointment to the Bench at the intervention of a peer who found this a convenient way of repaying a debt. Once established in his country jurisdiction, Justice Gobble, "a little, affected, pert prig," made a practice of holding court in his own house, hearing his cases in a crimson velvet nightcap with his wife sitting beside him to spur him on to malice and cruelty. Gobble "committed a thousand acts of cruelty and injustice against the poorer sort of people who were unable to call him to a proper account [and] was the subject of universal detestation."[3]

Even the Assize judges, those who travelled the country on circuit to preside at the trials of more serious cases and who sent hundreds to the gallows and many hundreds more to the colonies, were not above suspicion of corruption themselves. An episode, which became famous amongst lawyers for the manner in which it was reported, concerned Chief Justice Sir Thomas Richardson who was widely reputed to have given £17,000 for his appointment by James I. The case referred, in the legal jargon of the time, to a suitor in his court who "Ject un brickbat a le dit justice que narrowly mist." Richardson, at whom the missive was aimed, was bent over his desk at the time, and was heard to quip, "If I had been an upright judge, I had been slaine."

After a period of more or less honourable if repressive administration of justice during the Interregnum (1649-1660), the system quickly reverted to the old ways with the Restoration of Charles II who appointed judges at his pleasure — and removed them at a whim. These time-servers survived for as long as they carried out the King's wishes, principal amongst them the notorious Judge Jeffreys, though Charles had voiced the opinion that he had "no learning, no sense, no manners and more impudence than ten carted street-walkers."[4] Bishop Burnet wrote of him: "All people were apprehensive of very black design when they saw him made Lord Chief Justice, who was scandalously vicious and was drunk every day."[5] It was Jeffreys who, at the infamous "Bloody Assizes" of 1685 sought to earn the King's approbation by sentencing 330 rebels to the gallows and another 800 to transportation to the Americas. The fact that fewer than half were finally deported owes nothing to any clemency on Jeffreys' part. Against this man it was alleged that he took bribes for allowing prisoners to escape or for procuring their pardons. Though the evidence for this is contradictory, it is well established that he pocketed £14,000 for securing the pardon of Edmund Prideaux following his arraignment for high treason. He invested the proceeds in an estate which was known by some wags thereafter as *Hakeldama* or "field of blood."

But even a man as vilified as Jeffreys was capable of coming down heavily on the side of the angels. When his "Bloody Assizes" took him to Bristol he terrorised the local merchants and magistrates for their evil practices. One biographer wrote of this occasion:

> It is remarkable that there [in Bristol], all men that are dealers, even in shop trades, launch into adventures by sea . . . A poor shopkeeper that sells candles will have a bale of stockings or a piece of stuff for Nevis or Virginia and, rather than fail, they trade in men; as when they sent small rogues taught to pray [for transportation] and who actually received transportation even before any indictment [was] found against them.

> There had been a usage among the aldermen and justices of the city where all persons, even common shopkeepers, more or less trade to the American plantations, to carry over criminals who were pardoned with condition of transportation, and to sell them for money. This was found to be a good trade; but, not being content to take such felons as were convicts at their Assizes and Sessions, which produced but a few, they found out a shorter way which yielded a greater plenty of the commodity. And that was this. The Mayor and the Justices, or some of them, met at their tolsey (a court house by their exchequer) about noon, which was the meeting of the merchants as at the Exchange in London; and there they sat and did justice business that was brought before them. What small rogues and pilferers were taken and brought there and, upon examination, put under terror of being hanged, in order to which mittimus's were making, some of the diligent officers attending instructed them to pray transportation as the only way to save them; and for the most part they did so. Then no more was done; but the next alderman in course took one and another as their turns came, sometimes quarrelling whose the last was, and sent them over [to America] and sold them.[6]

Jeffreys formed the opinion that all the aldermen and justices of Bristol, "and the mayor himself as bad as any," were involved in this pernicious trade. Upon discovering that a small boy from one of Bristol's prisons had been illegally transported, he summoned the mayor, Sir William Hayman, to appear before him and to go down to the prisoner's post at the bar "accoutered with scarlet and furs." Jeffreys bawled across the court at him: "Kidnapper, do you see the Keeper of Newgate?" He then fined Hayman £1,000 and bound him and three others over in the sum of £5,000 to answer before the King's Bench to other charges of kidnapping the King's subjects for servitude overseas. But "the prosecution depended until the Revolution [of 1688] which made an amnesty, and the fright only, which was no small one, was all the punishment these juridical kidnappers underwent; and the gains acquired by so wicked a trade rested peacefully in their pockets."[7]

When King James II took flight from the country in 1688 to escape the vengeance of an antagonised populace, Jeffreys also feared reprisals against himself for the savagery of his treatment of Monmouth's followers in the west of England. Thinking to lay down his office, he surrendered the Great Seal of England to the King who threw it into the Thames, foolishly imagining thereby to impede the processes of justice after his escape. Jeffreys disguised himself as an ordinary sailor and hid on board a ship moored at Wapping, ready for his own flight overseas. But he was unwise enough the next day to go ashore to indulge his passion for drink in the Red Cow Inn, was recognised and surrounded by a crowd ready to do him violence. He sent to the Tower of London for an armed escort who marched him into confinement. When examined, he confessed his crimes but pleaded that his severity at the Bloody Assizes was far less than that demanded by the King. He died in 1689 from a stomach ulcer anointed with drink and was buried in the Tower.

Of his contemporaries, Robert Wright, whom Jeffreys himself appointed as a judge, was reported to the King as "a dunce, no lawyer, without truth or honesty, guilty of perjury and not worth a groat." With this recommendation behind him Wright, in turn, became Chief Justice but was charged in 1688 with taking bribes "to that degree of corruption as is a shame to any Court of Justice." He fled, was apprehended and committed to Newgate where, a few days later, he died from jail fever.

Even in this corrupt age, however, the judges and courts could be moved to extend such mercies as the savage laws allowed: reprieves were recommended for those found guilty on capital charges, and where truth was not hopelessly violated, the value of stolen goods was often written down to below a shilling to avoid the imposition of an automatic death sentence. During the seventeenth century fewer than three out of four persons sentenced to hang ever reached the gallows. In 1732 there were 502 indictments at the Old Bailey, 70 of whom were sentenced to death (some of these later acquitted), and 208 were transported. Of 240 felons convicted at the Old Bailey in London during 1755, only 39 were condemned to death and, of these, 10 were subsequently reprieved to be transported; 27 got off with minor punishment and the remaining 174 were sentenced to transportation. The law itself could also be turned to good account. By archaic custom any person convicted of felony in the seventeenth century could plead "benefit of clergy" and "call for the book." A specious theory derived from feudal times concluded that anyone who could read must be adjudged as being in holy orders and therefore exempt from capital punishment. If a felon, having "called for the book," was able to read the first verse of the fifty-first psalm beginning "Have mercy upon me, O God, according to thy loving kindness," he could be punished only by being branded upon the thumb or the shoulder. The illiterate were astute enough to memorise the vital lines and most judges felt able to turn a blind eye to the fact. This absurd practice was solemnly given recognition in an Act of 1705 accepting as valid a plea for benefit of clergy without proof of the ability to read, but at the same time it made many felonies such as murder, arson, burglary and theft "non-clergyable."

Mercy, too, could have its price. The Sheriff of London in 1675 advised the Lords of Trade and Plantations what it cost in fees to pardon a malefactor on condition of his transportation:

> *Item:* In searching the Record and drawing the Certificate for every prisoner pardoned; and for drawing the pardon in paper and afterwards ingrossing the same for the King's Majesties hand, and for the Allowance and entering the same upon Record   13s. 4d.

> *Item:* To the Clerk for ingrossing the Pardon for the Greate Seale for every person pardoned   2s. 6d.

> *Item:* To the Sword Bearer for every person pardoned
>   1s. 4d.

> *Item:* To Capt. Richardson the Jaylor and his man the Turnkey . . . each person   £1.11s. 0d.

> The Recorder of London saith, when there is a considerable
> number of these malefactors transported at each time, there
> is usually given unto his Clerke £5.[8]

The attitude of some judges to the draconian laws they were required
to enforce was well summed up in the course of a verbose and
sententious address delivered to the Grand Jury of Middlesex by its
chairman, Whitlock Bulstrode, Esq., shortly after the passing of the
Transportation Act of 1718. He admonished his colleagues:

> You are to present all parishes that have not stocks, whipping
> posts and cages in them. The want of this last occasions very
> often great expences to parishes remote from hence, and some-
> times the Escape of Criminals while the Facts are under Examina-
> tion . . . No nation under Heaven has better Laws than we have;
> besides, we have every Session of Parliament new Laws made
> to redress emergent evils; but yet the Nation is but little amended
> by them. What is the reason of it? 'Tis because the Laws are
> not duly put in Execution. Foreigners may justly complain that
> our Laws are very numerous and ill executed, which is a reproach
> to the Nation.[9]

As the century progressed, however, and more humanitarian views
came to prevail, more and more opportunities began to be taken of
tempering the strict demands of justice. It is remarkable, for example,
how many petitions presented by criminals under sentence of death
or transportation, during the last decade in which the 1718 Act
operated, were sympathetically received and acted upon. Judges
throughout the country were plagued by frequent requests from the
Secretaries of State to consider grounds on which sentences might
be favourably reviewed and, to their credit, many appear to have
gone out of their way to oblige. There remains the suspicion that
literacy, affluence or good connections could achieve for a condemned
person what merit could not, but very few of those who petitioned
against their sentences failed to gain a sympathetic hearing. One
example will suffice.

At the York Assizes in 1774 a young man named William Birch
was tried and sentenced to be transported for stealing sheep. A Dr.
Kaye immediately appealed on his behalf and the Assize judge, Mr.
Justice Blackstone, was required to comment on his decision. He
wrote:

As to the poor criminal at York, Dr. Kaye has represented very justly the nature of his offence and the circumstances of his family but is a little deceived as to his personal character, to which he indeed called some witnesses who spoke very coldly upon that head. The ewe and lamb [which Birch was alleged to have stolen] were taken off a Commons where the prisoner himself kept sheep so that they might have been taken by mistake. But, before he sold them as his own, he had clipped the ears and plucked the wool off the sides to take out the owner's marks, which militates against that supposition. Upon the whole I thought it not a case deserving of either capital punishment or impunity and have therefore recommended him to His Majesty for transportation for seven years. But if Lord Suffolk [a Secretary of State] has a wish to extend that mercy still farther, or to oblige our friend Dr. Kaye (whose nice feeling I am not unacquainted with), I do not by any means desire to obstruct the Royal Favor, nor do I think it a case of such very great guilt or notoriety that any prejudice can result to the Public from granting William Birch a free pardon.[10]

In the nick of time Birch was taken from the transport ship *Rebecca* and set at liberty, perhaps to reflect that for much lesser crimes many hundreds before him had suffered transportation without appeal.

NOTES

1. Henry Fielding, the grandson of a judge, first practised with no great success on the Western Circuit. He is generally credited with having organised the force which later became known as the Bow Street Runners, London's first efficient police system.

2. Alexander R. L. Melville, *The Life and Work of Sir John Fielding* (London, 1935), pp. 34-35.

3. *Adventures of Sir Launcelot Greaves* (London, 1793), pp. 221-237.

4. Gilbert Burnet, *History of His Own Time*, ed. Martin J. Routh (1833), (Hildesheim, 1969), Vol. 2, p.389.

5. *Dictionary of National Biography*, ed. Sir Leslie Stephen and Sir Sidney Lee (London, 1937-1938), Vol. 10, p. 715.

6. Roger North, *Lives of the Norths* (London, 1826), Vol. II, p. 24 ff.

7. *Ibid.*, Vol. I, p. 250.

8. PRO (Public Record Office): Colonial Office Papers, CO 324/4/30-31.

9. *Historical Register* (1718).

10. PRO: State Papers Criminal, SP 44/91/349 and 360.

CHAPTER IV

The State Monopoly – Early Days 1611-1718

The notion of augmenting the numbers of labourers in the English colonies by recruitment from the ranks of the prison population and undeserving poor is as old as the foundation of the colonies themselves. Richard Hakluyt, the Elizabethan explorer, may probably be credited with fathering the idea in his homeland when he wrote in 1584, drawing attention to "the multitude of idle and mutinous persons within the realm . . . whereby all the prisons are stuffed full" and recommending that "the pety theves might be employed for certain years in the western parts in sawing and felling of timber and in planting of sugar canes."[1] An Elizabethan Act of 1597 "for the Punyshment of Rogues, Vagbonds and Sturdy Beggars" appears to have been the first piece of legislation which specifically sanctioned the transportation overseas of rogues and vagabonds, and in 1606 Virginia was first recommended as "a place where idle vagrants might be sent."[2] Certainly from the time of the earliest English settlement in Virginia, reprieved felons worked side by side with free planters.

Spain, the other great colonising power of the time, being suspicious of England's intentions in the New World, sought advice from its Embassy in London about the flow of emigrants and received this reassuring reply: "Their principal reason for colonisation is to give an outlet to so many idle and wretched people as they have in England."[3] In this matter, at least, the Spanish envoys in London appear to have accepted the official line that the English expeditions to the new colonies were despatched, not against the interests of Spanish colonists but, in the words of Sir John Popham, "In order to drive from here thieves and traitors to be drowned in the sea."[4] Gondomar, the Ambassador of Spain to the Court of St. James, embellished his despatches home with a few lively pieces of tittle-tattle to reinforce the point:

A few days ago, he reported, when they were about to hang some thieves, three of them, the soundest and the strongest, were chosen to go to Virginia. Two of them accepted but the third would not, and seeing the two return to gaol, he said: "Let them go there and they will remember me!" Then he urged the hangman to shorten his work, as if he were thus relieved of a greater evil, and thus it was done.[5]

The opening up of the New World, and the prospect of new wealth with which it tempted its colonisers, coincided happily, from their point of view, with growing concern at home with what was considered to be a desperate increase in population and attendant poverty far beyond the power of the existing Poor Laws to contend with. The biggest problem standing between the directors of the Virginia Company and the clearing of new plantations by cheap labour was the broad expanse of the Atlantic and the cost of frequent crossings. There was a dearth of suitable volunteers. Those who could afford the crossing were unlikely, except to escape persecution or the results of their follies at home, to invest in so perilous an undertaking, or to stake their all on a speculative venture in a far distant and reputedly savage land. The agricultural labourer and artisan, however hard their lot in England, would certainly not face the terrors of a long and hazardous sea voyage in a time when an overland journey to London was an adventure to be boasted of. Propagandists were hired by the Virginia Company to present the new plantations in such glowing terms that credulity must have been greatly strained.

Broadsides issued by the Company solicited "workmen of whatever craft they may be, men as well as women, who have any occupation." Those who were prepared to go as colonists were promised £12.10s for making the voyage, houses to live in, vegetable gardens, food and clothing at the Company's expense, as well as "a share of all the products and profits that may result from their labour, each in proportion, and they will also secure a share in the division of the land for themselves and their heirs for evermore." The Company wrote to the Lord Mayor of London offering "one hundred acres for every man's person that hath a trade or a body able to endure days labour." The Providence Company went one better and began to organise a flow of letters from newly-settled colonists speaking enthusiastically of their improved conditions. Many were indeed lured by such unprecedented generosity, but news out of Virginia of hardship, famine, Indian savagery and brutal government quickly brought the propagandists' claims to naught. With the later introduction of the *headright* system, whereby planters already established in the colony were granted additional lands in proportion to the number of new settlers they imported, the way was open for private landlords to enrich themselves without the necessity of passing on any benefit to their hired labourers.

Forced labour in the colonies — indistinguishable in practice from slave labour — was quickly seen as a multiple blessing. Seen from England it alleviated the problem of over-population with the gratifying dividend of permanently removing the worst elements in the country; pressure on overcrowded jails and penal institutions was dissipated, and the heavy expense of poor relief mitigated. From the planter's viewpoint here was an abundant and unfailing source of free labour to be provided by able-bodied men, women and children to whom he had no contractual obligations during their term of service, and who might reasonably expect to be dependent on his goodwill thereafter. This happy resolution did, however, require some colour of legality, for even an ignorant Englishman was traditionally aware of his rights under the law. No existing statute countenanced forced labour in the colonies (as opposed to deportation) as a penalty for idleness or misdemeanour. Something was now required that would transmute mere banishment into a punishment with greater purpose. Whether or not inspired by Governor Dale's plea from Virginia to the King in 1611 to "banish hither all offenders condemned to die out of common goales, and likewise to continue that grant for three years unto the colonie [for] it would be a redie way to furnish us with men, and not allways with the worst kind of men," on 23 January 1615 the Privy Council issued the following warrant:

> Whereas it hath pleased his Majestie, out of his singular clemencie and mercie, to take into his princelie consideracion the wretched estate of divers of his subjectes who, by the lawes of the realme, are adjudged to dye for sundrie offences, though heinous in themselves yet not of the highest nature, so as his Majestie, both out of his gratious clemencie, as also for divers weightie consideracions, could wishe they might be rather corrected than destroyed, and that in their punishmentes some of them might live and yeald a profittable service to the commonwealthe in partes abroad where it shalbe found fitt to employe them [any six or more members of the Council are empowered] to reprive and stay from execucion suche persons as now stand convicted of anie robberie or fellonie (wilfull murther, rape, wichecraft or

burglarie onelie excepted) who for strength of bodie or other
abillities shalbe thought fitt to be employed in forraine discoveries
or other services beyond the seas . . . with this spetiall proviso,
that if any of the sayd offenders shall refuse to go, or yealding
to goe shall afterwardes come back and retourne from those places
where they are or shalbe sent or employed before the time limited
by us, his Majestie's Commissioners, be fully expired, that then
the sayd reprivall shall no longer stand, not be of anie force, but
the sayd offender shall from thenceforthe be subject to the execucion of law for the offence whereof hee was first convicted.[6]

There follow the names of seventeen prisoners to be recipients of
the King's clemency by being delivered to Sir Thomas Smith of the
Virginia Company.

A few years later, on 6 November 1619, these provisions were
extended and confirmed by a further order from the Privy Council:

Whereas there are divers prisoners in and aboute the citty of
London, as also in other parts of this realme, convicted of
felloneys, and for their said offences condempned by the law to
die, whoe being persons of able boddies fitt for labor may be
usefully imployed for the greate benifitt and service of the commonwealth, and to that ende may be constrayned to toyle in such
heavey and painefull workes as such a servitude shalbe a greater
terror to them than death it selfe, and therefor of better example
since execucions are so common as that wicked and irreligious
sorts of people are no way thereby moved or deterred from
offending . . .

It was therefor humbly moved by their Lordships that his Majestie
would be graciously pleased, out of his singular clemencie and
mercie, and to save the lives and perhaps the soules of a greate
many of his subjectes as thus wilfully runn into their own per-
dicion, to reprieve them from execucion of death (although it
may be contrary to their owne eleccion and will) so many of
them now being or hereafter to be condempned as shalbe humbly
recommended unto his Majestie's grace by the Lordes of his
Privey Councell, or by any six of them, upon certificate to their
Lordships from one or more of the judges or sarjantes at law
before whom such felones have ben tryed, or in their absence,
from two such principall commissioners before whom such fellons
have ben tryed, that they are of able boddies and stand convicted
of fellonie, and not for any murther, treason, rape, witchcraft,
robberie upon the high way, burning of houses, nor burglaries;

and the said persons so reprieved, some of them to be sent abroade
into forraine collonies and plantacions according unto the com-
ission and authority which his Majestie hath already given [an
apparent reference to the 1615 Order] . . . and some of them to
be imployed at home as aforesaid upon manuall labors and to be
kept in chaynes in the houses of correcion or other places as
shalbe thought fitt, with food and rayment as shalbe for necessitie
of life and no more; and that if afterwardes it shall appeare that
any of them, by his future demeanure and penitence for his former
faultes, shall deserve his Majestie's pardon, his Majestie may
then be pleased, upon sufficient certificate thereof and securitie
to be given for his good behavior afterwardes, to extend his
clemencie further and graunt him his gracious pardon; otherwise
to keepe them all under the sworde of justice and to cutt them
off when his Majestie shall please.[7]

This edict does not beat about the bush. The able-bodied felon
might hope to survive but the infirm were best despatched quickly.
Punishment was intended to be cruel, and little difference is drawn
between labour in the plantations and chain-gang service at home.
No wonder that the order specifically excluded the option of dying
on the gallows rather than submission to a bestial survival.

Few authoritative voices were raised against the new practice of
criminal transportation, and those that *were* could safely be ignored.
The foremost English philosopher of the day, Francis Bacon, in a
letter of 1616 to George Villiers, one of the King's favourites, wrote:

If any transplant themselves into Plantations abroad who are
known for schismaticks, outlaws or criminal persons, that they
may be sent back upon the first notice: such persons are not fit
to lay the foundation of a new colony.

He reinforced this view in his essay *On Plantations* in 1626:

It is a shameful and unblessed thing to take the scum of people,
and wicked condemned men to be the people with whom you
plant. And not only so but it spoileth the plantation. For they
will ever live like rogues, and not fall to work, but be lazy, and
do mischief, and spend victuals, and be quickly weary . . .[8]

But the State, having acquired a taste for this cheap and convenient
method of ensuring overseas expansion, was already casting around

for additional ways of recruiting human labour for deportation. It plumbed a new depth in sanctimonious and ruthless expediency when, on 31 January 1620, the Privy Council promulgated another order:

> We are informed that the City of London, by Act of Common Council, have appointed 100 children out of the Multitudes that swarm in that place, to be sent to Virginia, there to be bound apprentice with very beneficial conditions for them afterwards; and have yielded to a levy of £500 for the apparelling of these children and the charge of their transportation. Whereas the City deserves thanks and commendation for redeeming so many poor souls from misery and ruin and putting them in a condition of use and service to the State . . . and that, among their number there are divers unwilling to be carried thither, and that the City wants authority to deliver, and the Virginia Company to receive and carry out, these persons against their will; We authorise and require the City to take charge of that service to transport to Virginia all and every the aforesaid children. And if any children disobey or are obstinate we authorise the imprisonment, punishment and disposal of them; and so to Shipp them out to Virginia with as much expedition as may stand with convenience.[9]

The great livery companies of the city were called upon by the Lord Mayor each to contribute to this worthy cause, and they appear to have done so with alacrity. No protest was recorded, no champion of the oppressed challenged the legality of such an inhuman edict.

Where the State had led the way, private enterprise was not slow to follow. There was a ready cash market for any able-bodied man, woman or child who could be persuaded, cajoled, bullied or *spirited* to the new colonies. The fact that the euphemistic term *spiriting* was introduced into legal jargon to describe this particular form of kidnapping betrays the frequency of the practice. In 1649 "Spirits" were described as those who

> take up all the idle, lazie, simple people they can intice, such as have professed idlenesse, and will rather beg than work; who are perswaded by these Spirits they shall goe into a place where food shall drop into their mouthes; and being thus deluded, they take courage and are transported.[10]

By the mid-seventeenth century Parliament felt obliged to take more determined action against the practice by issuing a strongly-worded ordinance: "Whereas the Houses of Parliament are informed that divers lewd persons go up and down the City of London and elsewhere and in a most barbarous and wicked manner steal away many little children," justices were instructed to become very diligent in apprehending the culprits who were to be imprisoned and given exemplary punishment. The ordinance was to be read in every church of the land "that it may appear to the World how careful the Parliament is to prevent such Mischiefs, and how far they do detest a Crime of so much villany."[11] Parliament was, perhaps, more concerned with its public image than with the correction of this glaring abuse, for the practice of spiriting continued and increased with little evidence to suggest that local magistrates stirred themselves unduly to enforce the new edict. In Middlesex, the county in which spiriting was most prevalent, there is a striking absence of verdicts and sentences relating to kidnapping. Where fines *are* recorded, they often tended to be laughably trivial, sometimes a mere shilling. It has been suggested, on excellent authority,[12] that the kidnappers, when they were caught in the act of shipping children to Virginia, were often not brought to trial at all but allowed to compensate their prosecutors with money. In the courts of the metropolis the theft of a horse merited much stiffer penalties than the theft of a person.

Early in the seventeenth century the process of reprieving and transporting felons was somewhat vague and haphazard; it is even questionable whether candidates for the colonies were reprieved from death before or after they had been selected for service. One of the first to be named as a potential recruit was Stephen Rogers, condemned to death at the Middlesex Sessions in 1617 for killing a man but reprieved to be sent to Virginia at the intervention of Sir Thomas Smith "because he is of the Mystery of the Carpenters." The implication is that, but for his useful trade, he would have been hanged with his fellows in crime. Occasional warrants are to be found in Privy Council papers directing the release to the King's favourites of specified numbers of prisoners from English jails to be transported to the colonies. As often as not those so snatched from the gallows remain anonymous, such as the "twentie people, either all women, or half men and half women," whom Sir Thomas Smith was authorised to take into his care in 1620 for shipment to the Somers Islands.[13]

It was left to the reforming zeal of the victorious Parliament after the Civil War in England not only to introduce some order and regularity into the business of deporting undesirables but also to define new categories of people who might thenceforth be regarded as transportable. The first and obvious victims were to be those defeated in battle. On 28 July 1651 Rev. John Cotton wrote to Oliver Cromwell to inform him that "sundry" (i.e. 150) Scots captured at Dunbar in the previous year had arrived at Boston, New England, and had been sold "not for slaves to perpetual servitude but for six or seven or eight years." These were probably the prisoners who were ordered by the Council of State in November 1650 to be delivered to Augustus Walker, Master of the *Unity*, to be transported to New England. In September 1651 another 300 prisoners, this time from Worcester, were shipped by the *John and Sarah* to New England where they arrived the following spring. The use of New England as a destination for deportees marked a signal departure from established practice for, until now, only the southern colonies of America or the West Indies had benefited from white slave labour. The reason for establishing this precedent becomes clear when we read that the transportation of 900 further Scottish prisoners to Virginia, already put in hand in 1650, was stayed "till assurance be given of their not being carried where they may be dangerous." In 1650 Parliament forbade trade with Virginia for the colony's rebellion and did not accept its surrender until 1652.[14]

Once prisoners of war could be labelled as "rebels" they became fair game for transportation, and it was only a short and logical step then to bracket them with any political opponents of the regime, idlers, beggars and other shiftless nuisances. In short order transportation became the convenient method of disposing of all manner of undesirables and non-partisans, even of prisoners who had not formally been convicted. In 1653 Richard Netherway of Bristol was licensed to ship 100 "Tories" from Ireland to be sold as slaves in Virginia, their only crime being their political sympathies.

An irresolute rising against Parliament which took place in Salisbury in 1655 was crushed with the now customary severity. Those who had the opportunity and wit concealed themselves until they could flee overseas. Those that were taken prisoner were, on the direct orders of Cromwell, proceeded against with the utmost rigour. Some were executed and others reprieved in order to be sent as slaves to Barbados where they received such harsh treatment that few ever returned.[15]

To illustrate the effectiveness of the Parliament's policy in banishing evil-doers, Major-General Whalley was able to boast in 1656: "I may truly say you may ride all over Nottinghamshire and not see a beggar or a wandering rogue." He defended the policy stoutly:

> A better work for the safety and satisfying the country cannot be . . . Consider how the gaols may be delivered for the ease and safety of the countries [i.e. counties] . . . Horse stealers, robbers and other condemned rogues lie in the gaols. To continue them there is a charge to the country; to give them liberty there is to make more; and this long forbearing them without sending them beyond the seas I fear hath increased their number to the dissatisfaction of the country.[16]

In much the same strain Major-General Butler wrote in that year:

> Please to help me to a vent for those idle vile rogues that I have secured for the present . . . being not able to provide security for their peaceable demeanour, not fit to live on this side some or other of our plantations. I could help you to two or three hundred at 24 hours' warning, and the countries would think themselves well rid of them.

Butler made it clear that many of those he had in mind for transportation to the colonies had had no judicial trial. The complaint against three of them was that they had no employment or profession and were "very drunken fellows and quarrelsome, and are all single men fit for the service beyond the seas;" another "hath wandered up and down this twelvemonth [and] hath gone a wooing to two maids in this country and got monies of them;" two more were "suspected to live only upon the highway, keeping each a good horse and pistols and having no estate at all, nor following any calling." Against other of his detainees he charged such offences as keeping a lewd house, swearing, wife-beating, forgery, drunkenness, profane jesting and "scandalous filthiness."[17]

But Cromwell and his Council, perhaps conscious that these calls for yet more breaches of the rule of law, however popular they might prove in these cases, would have evil consequences, did not act precipitately. In the summer of 1656 a single order was given, and that only for the county of Surrey, to transport those persons who had been reprieved there. In preparation for more considered measures, however, all districts were then ordered to send in lists of dangerous persons, rogues and vagabonds recommended for transportation.

With these lists before them, the officers of State were now able to prepare a systematic and formal procedure for reprieving condemned prisoners on condition of their being transported. The new system borrowed heavily from the old but was careful to protect the forms of legality. To complement existing legislation, and no doubt to appease the Major-Generals, an Act was introduced in June 1657 requiring "idle and wandering persons" to give sureties for good behaviour to justices of the peace, and if they were unable (which was inevitably the case with many poor people), they became liable to appear at Quarter Sessions and to be transported for seven years. The formal practices ushered in by the Puritans for reprieving and transporting felons endured, virtually unaltered, until the start of the American War of Independence.

The accession of King Charles II in 1660, followed by a year of amnesty, served only to exacerbate the problem of what to do with the army of undesirables, much increased in the aftermath of civil war, economic distress and displacement. The uglier forms of nepotism and private enterprise so endemic under Stuart rule began to emerge again; the merchant class once more cast longing glances at the growing prison population as a potential source of new revenue. After a decent interval had elapsed — but no more — Jeremy Bonnell & Co. of London, in June 1661, petitioned the King to be allowed to take delivery of prisoners whom they would ship to Jamaica by their vessel, the *Charity*. But bureaucratic problems at once arose. The Lord Chief Justice was too preoccupied to consider such a minor matter, and the Recorder of London, to his credit, declared that he could not release any of his prisoners without a warrant from the King. So once more pardons on condition of transportation began to be issued and, in 1662, an "Act for the Better Relief of the Poor of this Kingdom" authorised the apprehension of any rogue, vagabond or sturdy beggar and made it "lawful for the Justices of the Peace in any of the Counties . . . to cause [them] to be transported as shall be duly convicted and adjudged to be incorrigible."

The sheriffs of London soon complained of the large expense they had to incur by housing reprieved prisoners in their jails while they awaited shipment to the colonies. The city had to be reimbursed by allowing it the profits from the sale of twenty of its felons. Other debts and obligations were conveniently met from the same renewable source. In November 1664 the King informed the sheriffs of London that Sir James Modyford was to have the privilege of taking all the pardoned felons from all the jails of England for a period of five years so that he might send them to his brother, Sir Thomas Modyford, "to improve the island of Jamaica." Notwithstanding, an identical licence was given to Thomas Bennet, son of Sir Humphrey Bennet, a year later; and in 1668 a Peter Pate was granted the exclusive trade in Newgate convicts.

The lack of discrimination shown by James II in disposing of reprieved felons by giving them to his favourites drew down upon him protests even from the notorious Judge Jeffreys, who wrote:

> I received your Majesty's commands . . . about the rebels your Majesty designs for transportation, but I beseech your Majesty that I may inform you that each prisoner will be worth £10 if not £15 apiece, and that if your Majesty orders them as you have already designed, persons that have not suffered in your service will be continually perplexed with petitions for recompense for sufferers as well as rewards for servants.[18]

His efforts were in vain for James continued to distribute pardoned felons between his Queen and his favourites including Sir William Stapleton, Governor of the Leeward Islands. It has been estimated that over 800 prisoners were disposed of in this way by James II and that less than half those chosen for transportation ever reached the West Indies; many died in prison and yet more failed to survive the sea passage.

Any hopes there may have been for greater tolerance, if not a relaxation, of the harsh penal code under the restored monarchy had received a rude shock within the first decade. Charles II and his ministers were not slow to adopt all the expedients for disposing of undesirables which had been devised by the Commonwealth, and now they set about improving and refining them. In 1663 the Westminster justices were authorised to arrange the transportation of five prisoners who had been remanded in custody as incorrigible rogues despite the fact that they had been found not guilty of the charges brought against them. The King's obsession "to repress the more than ordinary insolence of Quakers and other sectaries" was also soon translated into ruthless action to hunt down, evict, imprison and transport those whose conscience stood in the way of their conformity to the State religion. As well as the many Quakers who fled into voluntary exile before the wrath of the King, several hundred of their number who were either too poor or "stiff-necked" to follow them were rounded up and herded into confinement to await involuntary transportation at the King's pleasure. Those who were unable or who refused to pay the cost of their passage to the Americas were, in the chilling euphemism of the time, "to be employed as servants for seven years." Authority in law for their expulsion was introduced with the Conventicle Act of 1664 which expressly forbade their transportation to either Virginia or New England, where they might have hoped for some measure of sympathy. They were, therefore, shipped off to toil in the torrid sugar colonies. Nor were political deportees lacking, though at first fewer in number than Cromwell's thousands. After the suppression of an uprising in Scotland in 1678, the King ordered those responsible to be transported to Virginia, at the same time instructing his provincial officers to abrogate all Virginia laws which might have stood in the way of their importation.

The staple of the trade in human bondage, the scourings of the prisons in every English county, continued meanwhile in good supply. To keep pace with the handsome rate of capital convictions it soon became necessary to issue to most of the six Assize Circuits into which the country was divided a twice-yearly pardon on condition of transportation, while such pardons were needed even more frequently to cater for the burgeoning rate of imprisonment in Newgate. Reaction in the colonies to the continued dumping there of an increasing proportion of the English prison population, already a tender subject, grew from hostility to administrative action. Virginia, hitherto the most popular landing place, reached breaking point by 1670 when it was represented by three counties that "the peace of the Collony is endangered by the great number of fellons and other desperate villaines sent hither from the several prisons in England." It was recalled that some years previously "these villaines attempted the subversion of our religion, lawes, libertyes, rights and proprietyes [whereby] we lose our reputation whilst we are believed to be a place only fitt to receive such base and lewd persons."[19] The upshot was a prohibition on "any person trading hither to bring in and land any gaol birds or others who, for notorious offences, have deserved to dye in England." The colony wrote to the King complaining of "the great danger and disrepute brought upon this Plantation by the frequent sending there of felons," and informed him of the prohibition. A respite, to prove of short duration, was graciously allowed and the King gave instructions that felons were no longer to be sent to Virginia though emphasising that any other English plantation might be used.

One after another the American provinces came to experience Virginia's problems and began to close their ports to fresh consignments of English jail-birds. Difficulties then began to mount at home. In London pardoned felons awaiting transportation took full advantage of the confusion and the increasing laxity of their jailers. The inmates of Newgate seemed to roam about almost at will. A Commission of Enquiry reported in July 1682:

> Convicted prisoners in Newgate for some years past whoe have given Recognizance for transporting themselves upon his Majestye's gracious letters of pardon have not departed this kingdome according to the provisoe in the same expressed, but have remayned here . . . and committed new felonyes and offences and likewise increased their numbers as experience showeth; and alsoe by reason of the insufficiency of their manucaptors noe advantage can be taken of them. It is therefore ordered . . . that the provisoe in such like pardons for Convicts be drawne and made as formerly, and that the prisoners be transported by Merchants bound by obligation to his Majesty with good suretyes.[20]

Meanwhile a young man by the name of Christopher Jeaffreson, aware of the abundance of cheap labour available in London, set up in partnership with the Governor of St. Christopher's and one of the principal planters there, a Mr. Vickers, in order to begin the importation of convict workers. He reported to his principals on 4 September 1684:

> I hope to ship some malefactors after more difficulties than I imagined. I was opposed by the Recorder of London. I have to pay all the costs of prison fees and shipment, more than 40 shillings each. I was obliged to take 2-3 infirm men but they have trades. I hope they will fetch 400 lbs of sugar each.

This consignment appears to have discarded all their clothing before reaching the plantation but Jeaffreson advised that some part of the additional expense might be met by selling their shackles as old iron. He advised the Governor in April 1685 that he was arranging for a second consignment to be shipped by the *Friend's Goodwill*, under Captain James Foster, including "the women forced upon us [who] are a troublesome sort of merchandize." It was impressed upon Jeaffreson that he would have large penalties to pay if any convicts escaped, so he took personal control of the guard which escorted thirty-nine manacled convicts on Easter eve 1685 from Newgate to London Bridge where they were taken off by barge to the transport ship. Even so, they managed to commit many nuisances and to indulge in petty theft en route.

As soon as the convicts arrived at St. Christopher's, Jeaffreson's partners in the enterprise picked out the best men for their own plantations and allowed the weak, aged and sick to be allocated to their absent colleague. Jeaffreson was not disposed to continue the experiment.[21]

Clearly the system was beginning to creak and an overhaul was urgent. The State set itself to draft new rules and to tighten up those aspects of the administration which had failed. The Lords of Trade and Plantations recommended that a penalty bond of £100 a head (later reduced to £20) should be exacted in respect of all those pardoned for transportation so that they should serve in the plantations for at least four years; and the Recorder of London was ordered to ensure that felons in his custody, "good with bad," should be sent to those plantations which the terms of their pardons directed. The authorities, faced with evidence of past failures, appeared to lack any persuasive answer and all they could muster was a reproof to the Recorder of London for neglecting his instructions to keep women prisoners locked up until they were transported. Pressed for an explanation of his apparent laxity, the Recorder confessed in the autumn of 1697 that he had been unable to rid the capital of its summer collection of pardoned convicts, many of them now sick, "because the laws made in the plantations against receiving them" made it impossible. He undertook, perhaps a little rashly in view of the continuing difficulties, to do better in the future.[22]

The Government resolved, rather than allow more convicts, men or women, to be at large, that they would, in the last resort, subsidise their transportation. Seizing their opportunity, the Commissioners for Transports demanded the outrageous sum of £8 a head for shipping off the felons, upon which the Attorney-General was brought in to advise whether county sheriffs were not, after all, obliged themselves to arrange transportation of felons. In the end the Government had to resign itself to spending its own money since no merchant could be found willing or able to take the financial risk involved. As a stop-gap measure the Admiralty was ordered to provide shipping so that at least the women convicts might be carried away. The disposal of these women was presenting unusually severe difficulties. When their services were proffered to the colonies the lukewarm responses must have occasioned some long faces in London. "The entertainment of convicts is prejudicial," declared flatly the agent for Virginia and Maryland, adding that both provinces had passed a law which prevented their acceptance: "There is no proper place for them but Jamaica and Barbados." New England took its usual lofty line: "We have always desired to be excused, but the convicts will willingly be entertained by other colonies . . ." But the other colonies were also learning to show their muscle. Jamaica thought that women convicts were of no use there and would prove to be a burden. "We will not receive them unless we have 150 male convicts as well," was their final offer. Barbados was in full agreement: "They do not want women convicts for no Englishwomen work in the fields there and the people will not be willing to take them in their houses . . . but white women work in the fields in Virginia and Carolina and they will be acceptable there." So the buck-passing went on until New York offered a few crumbs of comfort by offering to accept women "if they are young and fit for labour;" Carolina, combining charity with caution, acquiesced but declared, "their reception is unknown but it will be better than elsewhere." The Leeward Islands, alone amongst those consulted, expressed no reservations about accepting the Newgate women. Gratefully the Government accepted their offer.[23]

By the beginning of the eighteenth century and with the business of transportation still in considerable disarray, war overtook the efforts of the administration to find an acceptable and permanent solution, and the war itself provided a partial remedy. From 1701 to 1712, while Marlborough, his English armies and their allies swept over Europe, some of their losses were made good by the conscription of able-bodied men from Newgate and other jails on condition that they served their terms either in the Army or the Navy. Their pardons were made out to exactly the same formula as had formerly been used to conscript plantation workers. Shipping was too valuable to the war effort to be spared for inessential cargoes. Now only the sick, the elderly and women unfit for hard work who crowded the prisons remained a problem. One of the Secretaries of State complained to the City of London in February 1706 that the women convicts pardoned for transportation were not able to bear the cost of their passage and that, even if merchants could be found to transport them, they would be unable to land them in the plantations because of the colonial laws forbidding it. He recommended, and the city accepted, that such women be put to hard labour in houses of correction.[24] The county of Middlesex, however, the principal source of convicted felons, was thought to be dragging its feet in implementing the new system. The justices of that county were gently reprimanded in February 1707 for continuing to seek ways of transporting women prisoners in Newgate and reminded that they should put them into houses of correction to work. Somewhat incensed, the justices retorted that their workhouse at Clerkenwell, having been built in 1663, could not manage to maintain itself even from the labours of the men housed there. The county had therefore enacted that none of their parishes, except one in Westminster, should be assessed for workhouses after September 1675 since they did not answer the purposes for which they were intended; and, unlike the City of London, there were no charities to assist. The Clerkenwell establishment in consequence stood empty and ruinous until it was let to Sir Thomas Rowe for £30 a year. By 1707 it had become quite incapable of receiving convicts.[25]

NOTES

1. Richard Hakluyt, "A Discourse on Western Planting," in *Collection of Voyages* (Edinburgh, Goldsmid edition, 1885-90), Vol. 13, p. 195.

2. Salisbury MSS, Hatfield: letter from Sir Walter Cope to Lord Salisbury.

3. Alexander Brown, *The Genesis of the United States* (New York, 1890), Vol. 1, p. 456.

4. *Ibid.* p. 46

5. *Ibid.* p. 476.

6. *Acts of the Privy Council of James I* (London, 1925), Vol. 2, p. 23.

7. *Ibid.* (London, 1930), Vol. 5, p. 53.

8. In the London Series of English Classics (London, 1889), Vol. II, pp. 10-11.

9. *Acts of the Privy Council of James I*, Vol. 5, p. 118.

10. William Bullock, *Virginia Impartially Examined* (London, 1649), p. 14.

11. *Acts and Ordinances of the Interregnum*, eds. C. H. Firth and R. S. Rait (London, 1911), Vol. I, p. 98 (No. 681).

12. J. C. Jeaffreson, *Middlesex Sessions Records*, introduction to Vol. IV, p. 11; *Virginia Magazine of History and Biography*, Vol. 83 (1975), No.3, pp. 280-287.

13. *Acts of the Privy Council of James I*, Vol. 5, p. 175: "Whereas his Majestie hath now under his pardon many condempned persons of both sexes and . . . is graciouslie inclyned to send them to some forrayne plantacion, and more particularly for the Sommer Islands, than here to suffer the law to take the forfeiture of their lives . . ."

14. *Calendar of State Papers, Colonial Series, 1574-1660* (London, 1860), p. 324 and p. 343.

15. *Diary of Thomas Burton* (London, 1828), Vol. 4, pp. 256-259.

16. Samuel R. Gardiner, *History of the Commonwealth* (New York, 1965), Vol. 4, p. 33.

17. *Ibid*. pp. 33-34.

18. George Bancroft, *op. cit.*, Vol. 2, p. 250.

19. Edward D. Neill, *Virginia Carolorum* (Albany, 1886), p. 328.

20. CLRO (Corporation of London Record Office): Sessions Book 6 July 1682.

21. Christopher Jeaffreson, *A Young Squire of the Seventeenth Century* (London, 1878), Vol. I, p. 159; Vol. II, pp. 123-126.

22. CLRO: Sessions Records for 1681/2; Repertory 101, f. 221.

23. The story of this bargaining with the several colonies is contained in the *Calendar of State Papers, Colonial Series* for May 1696-October 1697.

24. CLRO: Repertory 110, f. 68b and f. 75.

25. Middlesex Sessions Book No. 636 for 1707.

CHAPTER V

The Age of the Contractors 1718-1775

The return to conditions of peace after 1712 brought bubbling to the surface once more the thirty-year-old problem of how to rid the country's prisons, the Exchequer and the ratepayer permanently of the canker of a large, growing and expensive prison population. Hanging for major crime, which included the theft of property valued at one shilling or more, might resolve some part of the problem, but the real cause for concern was the swelling number of those whose poverty or natural inclination led them to commit petty crimes almost as a matter of course. The prisons could not be expected to hold them all.

A new and comprehensive solution had to await the disposal of even more pressing problems. The Scots rebelled in 1715 in support of James Stuart, the "Old Pretender," and the priority, after their defeat, was to rid the country of the many hundred prisoners who had been taken. Traditional measures were applied and rebels from this (and from the second Scottish uprising in 1745) were shipped off to the colonies. Parliament could now set its mind to a complete revision of contemporary law and practice governing the transportation of convicted felons. At one stroke a regular vent was to be supplied for all the English prisons, and the meddlesome attempts by the colonies to frustrate the importation of convict workers would finally be overruled.

Early in 1718 the Act for the Further Preventing Robbery, Burglary and other Felonies, and for the More Effectual Transportation of Felons passed into the statute book (text at Appendix III). The new plan of transportation hinged on finding a contractor who, at least cost to State funds, would provide a reliable and regular collection and shipping service. While the new Act was in the planning stage suitable talent was scouted. In 1716 a West Indies merchant, Francis

March, was found who agreed "to arrange for merchant ships bound for His Majesty's Plantations to receive at Gravesend all healthy malefactors to be transported and who will agree to serve in the plantations in America for eight years; and will transport them at his own expense." The British Treasury, in turn, agreed to deliver with each felon one pair of iron handcuffs and one pair of feet irons.[1] Despite his earlier undertaking, March was also paid forty shillings a head for the freighting of the felons while the Treasury was required to reimburse £170 to the Keeper of Newgate Prison for "passing a pardon" for fifty-four convicts and delivering them on shipboard. The Keeper's charges were itemised as:

> £4.1.0. for bread, beef, beer, brandy, cheese, etc. sent with 30 of the prisoners and their guard.
>
> £0.10.0. given to those prisoners who were almost naked.
>
> £32.8.0. for 54 hand and feet irons @ 12s. a head.
>
> £36.0.0. fees to the Clerk of the Peace for 54 persons @13s.4d. each.
>
> £40.1.0. fees to the Keeper @ 14s.10d. each.
>
> £10.15.0. for my own trouble and attendance four days in passing the pardon and 2 days and 2 nights in passing the prisoners.[2]

This first contingent of the new era sailed on the *Lewis* and the *Queen Elizabeth* to Jamaica. Some measure of the feeling aroused in that colony by the arrival of the new inhabitants may be gauged from the Governor's letter home of 1 September 1718:

> I think it my duty to acquaint your Lordships [of Trade and Plantations] that several people have lately been sent over out of the gaols in England upon the encouragement of an Act of Parliament . . . These people have been so far from altering their evil courses and way of living and becoming an advantage to us that the greatest part of them are gone and have induced others to go with them a pyrating, and have inveigled and encouraged several negroes to desert from their masters and go to the Spaniards in Cuba. The few that remains proves a wicked, lazy and indolent people that I could heartily wish this country might be troubled with no more.[3]

The evil consequences in the overseas territories from the new emphasis on transportation were not, from now on, to be weighed heavily against the obvious advantages to the mother country, though henceforth Jamaica, and soon the other West Indian colonies, were to be excused receipt of felons.

Redoubled efforts were now made to find a merchant who would permanently relieve the Government and the hard-worked justices, at least in London and the Home Counties, of the recurring burden of providing a shipping and disposal service for their convicts, and one who was reasonably honest, reliable and efficient. By July 1718 Jonathan Forward was promoting his claim to the post of "Contractor for Transports to the Government" through the Solicitor-General. His qualifications were impressive: he controlled a small fleet of ships engaged in the American tobacco and slave trade, had good connections in the Americas, and was well versed in the management of human cargoes. He proceeded shrewdly and engineered a sympathetic hearing from the Treasury by taking the first shiploads of convicts at his own expense. He then offered the Government a long-term contract whereby he would become responsible for transporting convicted felons throughout England at the rate of £3 a head, out of which he would himself meet jailers' fees of £1 a head, and felons from other parts (presumably Wales and Ireland) at £5 a head. He expressed regret at his inability to continue the provision of a free service, "considering death, sickness and other accidents." The Solicitor-General reported that there was no one else to be found to take the convicts at a lower rate and pointed to the advantages accruing to the public from "having the felons carried away each year."

On 8 August 1718 the Treasury and Jonathan Forward signed an agreement, renewed in 1721, to give Forward the effective monopoly as transportation contractor for twenty-four years. He set to work with a will and, within a year, had organised four ships to carry over 400 felons to Virginia and Maryland to be sold there to his own advantage. With this experience behind him, Forward now put the screws on the Treasury and in March 1719 demanded a higher rate for his services: £5 a head for felons from the county jails, but still retaining the old rate of £3 for Newgate prisoners. He gave as his reasons for demanding more that "tobacco, the usual produce of the felons, has been at a very low price . . . and he could not serve the public any longer by transportation at the present terms." Because

of the great number of felons then in jail awaiting transportation, the
Treasury was persuaded to agree to Forward's new proposals and to
award him a new long-term contract.[4]

At the same time as pressing for more lucrative terms, Forward
submitted his "Reasons for the more effectual transportation of the
convicts and felons," no doubt based on hard experience:

> 1. To make it Death for any Convict or Fellon that shall
> make their escape from on Board the Ship wherein he
> or she shall have been sent on board for Transportation,
> Except in case of Shipwreck.

> 2. If any convict or ffelon shall mutiny in order to run
> away with the ship or make their escapes it may be lawfull
> for the Captain and Ship's Company to punish the
> ringleaders of the said convicts or ffelons with death.

> 3. That if any person shall wittingly and willingly bring
> back any convict or ffelon to any part of Great Britain or
> Ireland before the time which they were transported be
> expired they shall forfeit £40 for every such person brought
> back to the informer that shall prosecute for the same.

> 4. That the prison fees for the convicts and ffelons be
> reduced to one third of what is now extorted for that a
> great deal of such offenders before the late Act was put in
> Execucion being hanged, they could receive no fees of them,
> and such as were branded and whipt were generally so poor
> that the jaylers usually turn'd them out of prison without
> paying fees, which said extortion being prevented will be
> a certainty to the merchants or contractors as well as an
> advantage to the Crowne.[5]

As might have been anticipated, the implementation of the 1718
Act produced teething troubles in some remoter parts of the country.
In June 1719 the first party of transports from Gloucestershire, eight
men and one woman, were taken by barge down the Severn to be
embarked on a ship for America. The Keeper of the City Prison
submitted a bill for £10.10s.0d. for his services which sent the justices
into an uproar. The committee which they set up to investigate a
more economical means of transporting criminals in the future determined that the transportation contractor should bear the whole cost
of maintaining the convicts from the date of their sentence. In other
counties the financial implications of the Act were carefully pondered

and many delayed the transportation of their felons for several years as an apparently cheaper option than paying their passage. The Common Council of Bristol in August 1723 was obliged to vote a sum of ten guineas to secure the pardons of women prisoners who had long languished at State expense in the city's jail because no person could be found who was willing to transport them: the same problem was experienced over twenty years later when a local transportation contractor refused to accept women prisoners for transportation.[6] In 1730 the Keeper of the County Prison in Salisbury was complaining of the excessive number of felons awaiting transportation who had remained for long periods under his charge because "no one else has concerned themselves" to pay their jail fees.[7] Nevertheless, with the machinery in place, the provisions of the Transportation Act eventually took proper effect throughout the country though, considering the hazards and atrocities involved in the traffic, the subject of transportation received little public notice. An occasional paragraph might appear in newspapers and magazines laconically informing readers of the number of prisoners most recently shipped to the colonies, but no writer of any consequence (except Daniel Defoe who relied on many underworld figures to provide material for his novels and had himself transported people to Maryland as a commercial enterprise) thought the subject of sufficient importance or interest to divert his attention. Only the Grub Street hacks, who made a precarious living by producing reports from the Sessions, largely for coffee-house circulation, which dwelt with special care on the more salacious and sanguinary crimes, found time to describe the trials of those who were transported. From time to time special editions would report, with a wealth of circumstantial detail, the spectacle of a public execution complete with a biography, last writings and dying words of those unfortunate wretches to whom no reprieve was granted.

The American colonies, sore at the cavalier way in which London had swept aside provincial susceptibilities and offended at the ever-swelling tide flowing towards them from the English prisons, continued their ineffectual protests. Hugh Jones, Rector of Jamestown, Virginia, was driven to complain in 1724:

> White servants are of three kinds: 1. such as come upon certain wages by Agreement for a certain Time; 2. such as come by indenture, commonly called *Kids*, who are usually to serve four or five years; and 3. those Convicts or Felons that are transported,

whose Room they had much rather have than their Company; for abundance of them do great Mischiefs, commit Robbery and Murder, and spoil Servants that were before very good. But they frequently there meet with the End they deserved at Home, though indeed some of them prove indifferent good. Their being sent thither to work as Slaves for Punishment is not a mere Notion, for few of them ever lived so well and so easy before, especially if they are good for any thing . . . [They] for the most Part, who are loose Villains, made tame by Wild [i.e. Jonathan Wild], and then enslaved by his Forward Namesake . . . if they forsake their Roguery together with the other *Kids* of the later Jonathan, when they are free, may work Day-Labour, or else rent a small Plantation for a Trifle almost.

The Servants and inferior Sort of People, who have either been sent over to Virginia or have transported themselves thither, have been, and are, the poorest, idlest and worst of Mankind, the Refuse of Great Britain and Ireland, and the Outcast of the People.[8]

Finding itself unable to resolve its problem by direct action, Virginia attempted more devious means in 1723. The colony proposed an Act requiring the masters of vessels to give bond not to allow convicts on shore until they were *bona fide* sold and for the good behaviour of such convicts after they were disposed of. On Forward's intervention, the Act was promptly disallowed by Whitehall as amounting to a prohibition on the importation of convicts and therefore in contravention of the 1718 Act of Parliament. As the review committee commented: "If this example were to be followed by other colonies, the practice of transportation would be rendered wholly impracticable."[9] And three years later Governor Gooch wrote to the Lords of Trade in London:

The secret Robberies and other villainous attempts of a more pernicious crew of transported felons are yet more intollerable: witness the dwelling house and outhouses of Mr. Thomas Lee which in the night time were sett on fire by these and other villains and in an instant burnt to the ground, a young white woman burnt in her bed . . . and this was done by those rogues because a Justice of the Peace, upon a complaint made to him, had granted a warrant for apprehending some of them.[10]

The Virginia Assembly decided that more severe penalties were needed against the growing practice of arson, and introduced them in an Act of 1730 "in a country which is so much crowded with convicts." The Governor was convinced that the Northern Neck, "being already turbulent and unruly . . . was not likely to become better by being the Place of all this Dominion where most of the transported convicts are sold and settled." By 1748 the Assembly had decided that transported convicts should receive less generous treatment than indentured servants on the grounds that they "may confer an Odium on this Country that we are like those we encourage, and honest men will not chuse to live in such company."[11]

Maryland scarcely fared better, to judge from the following record made by the Baltimore County court in August 1723:

> Whereas the great number of convicts of late imported into this Province have not only committed divers murders, burglaries and other felonies, but debauched several of its formerly innocent and honest inhabitants, and whereas there are very great numbers of the said convicts in this County which encourages them to be more frequent in the perpetration of their villainies . . . and expose several of the good people thereof to their insults and rapines besides putting the country to a vaste expense in prosecuting them for their crimes, all which renders it absolutely necessary to use all lawful means to protect the innocent from such wretches . . .[12]

Agents for Jonathan Forward complained in 1725 that two ships which had arrived in Annapolis loaded with convicts had been unable to discharge their cargo because the provincial authorities were insisting on a bond for the felons' good behaviour. Unwilling to take on such a financial responsibility, the agents had been obliged to receive the felons back on board ship. London reacted as it had to Virginia's efforts and disallowed any hindrance to the importation of convicts into Maryland.[13]

But it was left for Benjamin Franklin, in a savage and sarcastic article written in 1751 (text at Appendix VII), to suggest that some thousands of felons in America, whom he called rattlesnakes, might be rounded up and shipped to the elegant parts of London as an expression of gratitude for the convicts shipped from the mother country.

Pennsylvania followed Virginia's lead and attempted by local legislation to limit, if not to exclude, the immigration of convicted felons. The colony introduced Acts in 1722 and 1729 to impose a duty on the importation of "persons convicted of heinous crimes and

of poor and impotent persons." In this instance Whitehall was not
alerted until 1746 when the Pennsylvania legislature was imprudent
enough to submit the text of a further Act along the same lines. The
entire enterprise was immediately and heavily quashed as, in the
opinion of London's legal advisers, "likely to prevent the importation
of servants who might be of public utility in the improvement and
well peopling of the province."[14]

The complaints of the colonies were chiefly directed against the
evil disposition of imported felons, but another charge levelled against
the system was that it brought in a class of labourer quite unsuited
to plantation work. The Province of Georgia, wrongly conceived in
popular imagination to have been the principal recipient of deported
felons, commented in 1740:

> The Persons sent from England on the *Charity* were of the
> Unfortunate . . . [and] many also shewed they were brought to
> these Misfortunes by their own Faults; and when those who
> quitted their own Country to avoid Labour, saw Labour stand
> before their Eyes in Georgia, they were easily persuaded to live
> in Carolina by Cunning rather than work. This has been a great
> Misfortune also upon many Persons who brought over Servants
> indented to serve them for a certain number of years who, being
> picked up in the Streets of London, or some such Manner, their
> Masters found them unfit for Labour, and many of them took
> such Opportunities as they could to get to desert and fly into
> Carolina where they could be protected. Indeed, good and bad
> which came from England were mostly Inhabitants of Towns
> there; but such seldom turn out good Husbandmen with their own
> Hands; yet some of them proved very useful in a new Colony
> since they most readily compose Towns.[15]

Georgia wanted, instead of these townsfolk, English or Welsh servants
"who were strangers to London and used to hard labour in the
country."

Jonathan Forward's reign as Contractor for the Transports came to
an end when his twenty-four year contract expired and he was
succeeded on 4 February 1742 by one of his associates and fellow
London merchant, Andrew Reid. Under Reid, who held his post for
twenty-one years by contract, the business of transporting felons went
forward apace, but the new management soon allowed its devotion
to quick profits to subdue adequate supervision of the trade and even

that modicum of humanity which had formerly prevailed. Reid's partner and ultimate successor, John Stewart, wrote with more honesty than tact to the Treasury in 1762:

> The contract . . . was formerly in the hands of a person [i.e. Reid] against whom almost every species of complaint was made. However, he continued to execute this part of Public Justice above twenty years because, for the greatest part of the time, no one could be found to undertake it, few people being fit or caring for so perilous an exercise.

He was even more blunt about the way in which "the transporting of criminals is left to the lowest and most corruptible class of Public Officers."[16]

For a brief period in 1752 it looked as though the administration was having second thoughts about the wholesale deportation of convicts. The House of Lords pondered a Bill which might have drafted them into His Majesty's dockyards but "distinguished from artificers by chains and other marks of slavery and to receive corporal punishment for laziness and disobedience." This proposition evoked much vigorous protest on the grounds that the employment of unpaid and dishonest knaves would deprive honest workmen of their bread. Amongst the alternatives suggested were that convicted felons should be sent to work in the coal mines; be employed in repairing and maintaining roads in the north of the kingdom; or be exchanged for English slaves held in Morocco on the basis of two felons for one slave. But their Lordships rejected the Bill.[17]

Largely by self-recommendation, John Stewart in 1763 secured his succession to the post of Contractor for the Transports, though the Treasury were now prepared to offer only a short-term appointment and, upon Stewart's death in 1771, appeared determined to rid itself finally of the increasing burden of contractors' fees. It set afoot enquiries in the City of London about the possibility of disposing of convicted felons without any cost to the Exchequer. Stewart's business partner and heir-apparent as Contractor for the Transports was one Duncan Campbell (1726-1803) who traced his descent from the Glasgow family of that name. He was already prominent in the West Indies trade following his marriage in 1753 to the daughter of a wealthy Jamaica planter, and owned both plantations and ships including the *Bethia*, which later became famous as Bligh's ship, the *Bounty*. His kinsman, John Campbell, was the first captain of H.M.S.

Victory at the Battle of Ushant in 1778. As chairman of the London merchants trading to Virginia, Duncan Campbell was a man of considerable influence in the City of London and applied his position and power to retain the management of the transportation trade.

Battle lines were drawn between the Treasury and Campbell who, on the presumption of an official appointment, had carried on the trade for six months after his partner's death and had made commitments for many more months ahead. Hearing of the Treasury's new intentions, Campbell made known his anxiety and claimed £5 a head for 173 convicts he had shipped to America late in 1772. The Lords of the Treasury, already in receipt of more attractive offers from the City, replied icily to enquire Campbell's grounds for his claim: "We understand the contract has expired and transportation was left to the management of the Courts."[18] In January 1773 Campbell tried again, this time forwarding to the Treasury a certificate from the Committee of Virginia Merchants and others concerned in the tobacco trade which asserted: "Mr. Campbell must have lost £1885 by purchases of tobacco made by his agent for loading on to felon ships." Their Lordships continued to be unimpressed and demanded further proofs of Campbell's losses.[19]

The hard line taken by the Treasury was encouraged by the welcome discovery that certain Old Bailey magistrates had made themselves acquainted with "persons ready to transport felons without premium." Mr. Alderman Trecothick of the City of London went so far as to say that merchants in the Virginia and Maryland trade would even contend for a contract to export felons at their own expense. Evidence from London and Middlesex court records is that merchants were indeed as forthcoming here as they were in other parts of England to provide free shipping for convicts in anticipation of a good profit on their sale in America. Freebooting traders such as Abraham Moses Fernandes and Moses Israel Fonseca, who had less acceptable credentials even than the former official contractors, negotiated successfully for single shiploads of convicts.[20] But political events were now rapidly overtaking the trade.

Duncan Campbell, having finally won the agreement of Lord North, the First Lord of the Treasury, to his appointment as official transportation contractor, wrote the following dismal account in June 1776:

> I have saved the publick great expense for years past. I have not
> yet received one shilling profit by that Service but am in a very

large Advance on that Account; whether I shall ever receive any benefit depends on the value of American effects. Indeed Debts of such a Nature as those from Buyers of Servants are, from the Circumstances of the times, rendered more precarious than any other. The last ship I sent out to Virginia with convicts was compelled to depart [from Virginia] in Ballast and the servants might rather be said to be Landed there than sold, for I expect nothing from that Cargo. I foresaw in great degree what would happen in the course of this ship's voyage, but I was unwilling to show any Doubts at such a time.[21]

An era was coming to an end.

NOTES

1. *Calendar of Treasury Books 1757*, Vol. 30, pp. 578-579.

2. PRO (Public Record Office): Treasury Papers, T 53/25/224, 281.

3. PRO: Colonial Office Papers, CO 137/13.

4. *Calendar of Treasury Papers 1720-1728* (London, 1889), No. 9, p. 468.

5. PRO: Treasury Papers, T1/220/42.

6. John Latimer, *Annals of Bristol in the Eighteenth Century* (1893), p. 150.

7. PRO: State Papers, SP 36/20/45.

8. Hugh Jones (Minister of Jamestown), *The Present State of Virginia* (London, 1724), pp. 53-54, 114.

9. *Calendar of State Papers (Colonial) 1722-1723* (London, 1934), No. 613, p. 293.

10. Quoted from Fairfax Harrison, "When the Convicts Came," *Virginia Magazine of History and Biography*, Vol. 30 (1922), pp. 250-260.

11. *Ibid.*

12. Basil Sollers, "Transported Convict Laborers in Maryland During the Colonial Period," *Maryland Historical Magazine*, Vol. 2 (1907), p. 29.

13. *Ibid.*, p. 30.

14. *Acts of the Privy Council (Colonial) 1745-1766* (London, 1911), No. 28, pp. 20-23.

15. *A State of the Province of Georgia* (London, 1740), quoted in Peter Force, *Tracts Relating to the Origin, Settlement and Progress of the Colonies in North America* (Washington, 1836-1846), Vol. 1.

16. PRO: Treasury Papers, T1/416.

17. See letters in *Gentleman's Magazine*, Vol. 22 (1752), pp. 81, 325.

18. PRO: Treasury Papers, T1/514.

19. *Ibid.*

20. PRO: State Papers, SP 44/91/68 and 92/105.

21. PRO: Treasury Papers, T1/521.

CHAPTER VI

Transportation as a Business

Those who first profited from the transportation of convicts to the Americas during the seventeenth century were the colonisers themselves, then the King's favourites upon whom reprieved felons were bestowed as a gift, and finally the merchants and shipowners. These last would pick up what felons they could obtain from the prisons, transport them at their own expense, and sell them for the best price obtainable in the American or West Indian plantations. It was not until the passing of the Transportation Act of 1718 which established a uniform code of practice that it became necessary to treat the export of felons as a business in its own right, and for official contractors to be appointed who were equipped and able to dispose efficiently of a heavy traffic in human flesh. The terms of the Act made it clear that merchants with experience in the American trade would be needed and, almost inevitably, the choice would fall upon those who had ships already fitted out for the carriage of large numbers of people securely confined in the holds — i.e. those engaged in the black slave trade.

The first contractor appointed, Jonathan Forward, was well qualified in every respect. He was already by 1716 a successful City merchant who had made his name in general overseas trading and in the international slave markets. His ship the *Jonathan* plied regularly between London, Africa and the southern colonies of America. When she foundered at Antigua in 1717 "a great part of her cargo [black slaves] was irretrievably lost," and Forward was thereby in great need of a supplementary income which a Treasury contract promised to supply. That he was firmly entrenched also in the tobacco trade is evidenced from the various lawsuits in which he appeared, mainly as the assignee of tobacconists who went bankrupt. His interests in Virginia and Maryland were sufficiently established by 1718 for him to be nominated by the Customs Commissioners to recover on their behalf a debt from John Goodwin's estate in those provinces. His later involvement in the transportation of felons also brought him frequently into the law courts, for which there is cause to be grateful, since little other record of his activities throughout a long career remains.

On the first news of the new Act, Forward shrewdly tempted the Treasury into an exclusive contract by clearing Newgate of forty felons whom he transported at his own expense, then by taking two further shiploads at very low rates. This public-spirited generosity so captivated the Solicitor-General that he went on record as saying: "This is very cheap!" But his early ventures could hardly have filled Forward with enthusiasm. His first convict ship to Maryland, the *Dolphin*, owned and commanded by Gilbert Poulson, was fitted out for the trade at a cost of £375 and left London towards the end of 1717 with 134 felons aboard. On her arrival in the Patuxent River early in 1718 the 127 surviving "seven-year passengers" were sold and, almost immediately, Poulson, "much encouraged by the Governor," sued Forward in the local Admiralty court to recover sums allegedly due to him. The *Dolphin* was impounded and Forward's assets in Maryland, valued at £2,000, were seized. Lord Baltimore had discovered a new and ingenious way to obstruct the entry of an unwanted class of new immigrants. Forward made strenuous efforts to obtain redress, but litigation and appeals went ahead at a snail's pace. In August 1720 the Lords of Trade and Plantations brought themselves to order the restoration of Forward's goods in Maryland but, by then, Poulson himself had run into debt, had been imprisoned, and had then left the province altogether. Forward now sued the local officials responsible for the seizure of his property and was still prosecuting a seemingly interminable and hopeless cause in 1725 when he set off in person to Maryland to sue the Deputy Governor.[1] Meanwhile, the *Dolphin*, such was her condition, had sunk at her moorings because a cabin window was left open, and before she could venture to sea again, her main deck and quarter deck had to be rebuilt. Even then expert examiners declared that the ship was in no condition to carry a cargo back to England.

The voyage of another of his early ships, the *Eagle*, which Forward had selected as "most suitable to the purpose, being a Guinea ship" (i.e. one employed in the black slave trade), fetched him again into the law courts to be sued by her owners for payment of freightage.[2]

Forward had delivered 107 Newgate prisoners to Robert Staples, the *Eagle*'s captain, and concluded his business with him at a tavern in Gravesend, Kent, in September 1718 by paying him £3 a head for the convicts who were to be carried to Virginia and Maryland.[3] This was one of the voyages designed by Forward as a loss-leader to lure the Treasury into granting him a long-term contract. Since Forward himself had to pay all jail fees out of his own pocket, and received only £3 a head for this consignment from the Treasury, he was at great risk of losing money by paying Staples at the same rate. If his convicts came to a good market in America he could no doubt afford to take a temporary loss but, even so, he was not long in asking the Treasury for a higher premium of £5 a head.

Despite the difficulties and dangers of the new trade in convicts, it meshed in wonderfully well with the established tobacco interests: from America came ships laden with the new crop of leaf to be auctioned in London, Bristol, or Liverpool, and back went the same ships, this time crammed with felons to be auctioned to plantation owners in exchange for further supplies of tobacco. The risks were considerable for, quite apart from the normal hazards of a long sea crossing, the shippers had to contend with pirates, wars, the notorious jail fever and the ever-present threat of an uprising by desperate convicts. In 1720 the *Honor*, while on her way to Virginia, was taken over by fifteen mutinous felons who forced her captain, Richard Langley, to put them ashore at Vigo. Another consignment of convicts for Maryland embarked in 1724 in Jonathan Forward's newly acquired ship, another *Jonathan*, commanded by a new captain, Darby Lux,[4] may well have been responsible for the fire which broke out on board and sank her. In the same year John Jones, commander of the *Rappahannock*, bound for Virginia with felons, caught smallpox from his passengers and died in Falmouth outward bound.

In 1742 the *Forward*, under John Sargent, made what was to prove a disastrous voyage to the Potomac River. On her outward passage fifty-eight of the felons on board died and, on her return leg, the ship was taken prize by a Spanish privateer. Another convict ship, the *Mary*, was lost at sea in 1746 and, in that same year, the *Plain Dealer*, bound for America, was engaged by the French warship *Zephyr*. The convicts being transported rallied to assist in the action against the French but their efforts were unavailing and the *Plain Dealer* was wrecked on the French coast with the loss of most on board. In 1756 the *Bella*, commanded by William Middleton, sailed from Bristol carrying thirty-six male and fifteen female prisoners condemned by the judges of the Oxford Circuit to be transported. She was captured by the French who shipped the convicts to Spain and then overland to Lisbon where they "were guilty of many excesses." The British Consul in Lisbon complained to London and asked for the speedy removal of these embarrassing British subjects, while the French were ready to exchange them for their own prisoners-of-war. The proposal seems to have irritated Whitehall, which posed the question to its legal advisers: "Should they [the convicts], being an encumbrance to us, be an equivalent for useful subjects of France demanded in their stead?" The lawyers' answer was affirmative, so the convicts were shipped back to England in the man-of-war *Wager* and packed off again from Bristol in 1761 by the *Atlas* to complete their terms of servitude in Maryland.[5]

Nor were the risks confined to the sea voyage. In 1725 Jonathan Forward sued the Lord Lieutenant of Lincolnshire with whom he had contracted for the transportation of felons from Lincoln Castle at the rate of five guineas a head. The story that emerged at the trial of his suit was that the *William and Mary*, commanded by William Taylor, had been sent by Forward to the River Humber to fetch eighteen felons to London for transfer to the *Forward* which would transport them to America. On 5 October 1724 the felons overpowered Captain Taylor and his crew, threatened their lives, locked them in a cabin, and made their escape in the ship's longboat. The Lincolnshire authorities claimed that Taylor had been neglectful in having no more than two or three sailors on board his ship at a time when the felons "were not fettered, put under hatches, [or] secured or confined." They declared that "the country in general will probably sustain damage by having so many thieves let loose amongst them which they have, at their great expense, secured and convicted for example's sake."[6] The county had some success in recapturing the escapees for eleven of them were in November 1725 embarked for Virginia on the *Rappahannock* where a terrible revenge awaited them. The landing certificate for that ship issued in Virginia in April 1726 shows that only one of the recaptured convicts from Lincoln survived the passage of the Atlantic.

Having learned his lesson, Forward set about improving his security measures, but other problems were still to plague him. In January 1726 a Peter Casey of Holborn, Middlesex, brought a lawsuit against Forward seeking payment for his services as a factor, claiming that

"Forward gave great encouragement to supercargoes and factors because of the great danger to the ship's company when felons are transported and attempt to gain their liberty." Casey had applied to Forward in August 1724 for employment and was asked to take command of a ship, but he declined on the grounds that he had not been bred to the sea and had experience only as a merchant in Virginia and other plantations abroad. He was then offered the post as Forward's factor in Virginia at the same rate as was allowed to John Moal, the factor in Maryland — £100 a year plus expenses — but, to begin with, he must "be content with only half commission since the felons must be consigned conjunctively to . . . some inhabitants of the country better skilled in the method of vending and selling such felons." The men so skilled were named as Major George Braxton, Mr. George Tilly, and Mr. James Horsenail, each of whom received 7½ percent on all sales of felons which they made. Casey shipped as supercargo on the *Forward* in September 1724, having checked on board ninety-four felons and three covenanted servants. Of these Braxton was to receive ten, Horsenail twenty and Tilly sixty-seven, at an estimated sale value of £1,200. But as soon as the *Forward* arrived at Rappahannock, a report was put about that both the felons and the ship's company had the smallpox, so terrifying the inhabitants that they would not buy servants from this source "without incurring the displeasure of their neighbours." Casey went to see Major Braxton who lived sixty miles from Yorktown in order to seek his help but he refused to become involved and handed back the bill of lading for his servants, telling Casey to dispose of them somewhere else on the best terms he could obtain, "for several ships were expected there with Negroes from the West Indies which would prove very detrimental to the sale of the felons; and if Casey could not dispose of them readily for tobacco (which he apprehended to be next to an impossibility at that season of the year) he should sell them to the planters for tobacco payable in the following October rather than keep them any longer on board to eat out the ship's provisions." Casey made his weary journey back to Rappahannock River where both Tilly and Horsenail shut their doors against him. He was again told to dispose of the felons himself because the neighbourhood was terrified by the news of smallpox. Finally Casey appears to have disposed of his "servants," presumably at rather low prices, for his account shows that he received for the seventy-eight felons who survived the voyage and for the three covenanted servants 83,130 lbs of tobacco and £170.15s.0d. in local currency.

Forward's agents in Virginia gave their own version of what happened. In July 1725 James Horsenail wrote to his principal:

> I doubt not but I should have disposed of [the felons] in this part of the River had it not been for a report spread about that the smallpox raged among them so that none of the gentlemen in these parts would none of them go to the ship, nor suffer me to bring any of them up to their plantations. This obliged me to leave the affair wholly to Mr. Peter Casey and Mr. Tilly.

His account was supported by George Tilly who wrote at the same time:

> Thousands [*sic*] of people in Virginia durst not come near your ship on any account, by which means I writt to Mr. Casey to sell for tobacco at the full or anything, for they had no provisions left when they arrived, save about a barrel of beef. Mr. Casey and the Captain went to Court and offered to give their oaths that they had not the small pox since they came out of England, then the people did venture to buy on credit.

In the following month Tilly wrote again:

> Sir, I would have got all your effects out of Casey's hands but could not, he insisting that he would keep some in his hands for Commissions. . . I told him it was unhandsome to doubt your Honour in your payment to him for what you agreed . . . but I could not prevail. All I know he has in his hand are as followeth: Received of Co. Lomax for a servant £15; of William Dolten for a servant £9; of William Taylor £4.13; of William Robinson £4.14; of Saml. Edmondson £11.15.3. . . . He is also engaged for swearing ten oaths £2.10. He received for Mr. Bluett [*see chapter X for an account of this colourful rogue, William Blewitt*] freedom for what he agreed with him, for I do not know . . . I am afraid I shall be the greatest sufferer in respect of losing several gentlemen's consignments that had tobacco on your ship . . . Casey made a great many bad debts. . . If you approve of it, consign to me 100 felons by the first opportunity in the same ship without any person being concerned in partnership with the fellow [Casey]. I will do my best endeavours to sell your cargo and to load your ship, you allowing me 7½% for sales and returns. But you must have your ship well sheathed before you send her from London, and must send a careful Master that knows the charge of a shipload of tobacco, and I would have you give him something extraordinary to assist in the sales of your Servants.

And in a further note to Forward, who had "signified being a little in pain" about his ship:

> You have reason enough so to be, for I must be plain to tell you that the Master and Merchant would have spent your ship and sales if I had not supported them. . . Their extravagance was so great that I durst not venture to key [give] them any rum for the ship till she was ready to sail by the reason that they was in York and bought of Mr. Flower 100 and odd gallons; they never was sober hardly when they had it . . . They runned in 10 or 12 people's debt afterwards for rum, but have it they would, if it was to be had in Virginia. The Master and Merchant sold a servant to Dalton for £9, and that they spent, and Brockett pawned his watch for £1.9s.

In his last letter in February 1726 Tilly informed Forward:

> Casey made several bad debts. Two servants he sold to Doctor Clark, your ship's doctor. I have issued writs against him but the Officer cannot take him: he makes a Mint [i.e. a fortress] of his house, but I follow him up with attachments against his estate. I hope the debt will be recovered by this reason that he has married a wife with negroes. I hope that when your servants come in this year they will sell well by the reason that I have £50 bespoke. You may depend on it that I will take all the care that can be in getting in your debts and in the disposing of your servants.[7]

If agents and factors could line their pockets by blatant dishonesty, the ships' captains employed in the transportation business, already well versed in extortion by violence, as will be seen, were not above exercising their clerical skills to their own advantage. William Loney, one of the senior captains employed by Jonathan Forward between 1728 and 1737, had already retired to comfortable domesticity in Hatton Garden, London, when his artful swindles were discovered. Forward estimated that he had been cheated out of £1,400 by Loney's frauds which included switching the marks on hogsheads of tobacco so that he received good quality leaf and Forward the inferior kind. Loney was also well practised, as were some of the factors, in collecting his master's debts and applying them to his own uses. The accounts which Loney submitted in his defence included a statement of receipts from the sale of felons from the various ships under his command:

Year	Ship	Tobacco	Virginia Money	Sterling
1729	*Forward*	141,400		£37.7.3.
1730	*Forward*	181,878	£153. 0. 0.	
1731	*Smith*	115,263	4. 0. 0.	15.0.0.
1732	*Smith*	178,450	89. 3. 0.	
1733	*Caesar*	64,398	394.13.10.	
1734	*Caesar*	135,723	557. 7. 0.	
1735	*Caesar*	58,647	847.11. 9.	32.3.4.
1736	*Dorsetshire*	61,230	983.19. 6.	
1737	*Dorsetshire*	190,069	399.12. 6.	3.4.0.

Among his accounts appear such items as:

> 1735: To Chris. Robinson order by letter for a felon: £10
> (Va.)

> 1737: To Augt. Smith servt. taking away by his first
> Master: £10 (Va.) To abatement to several parsons
> their ballances by reason the felons was pox'd and
> some run away 2,000 tobacco.

> 1738: To Alex. Parker £3 for curing a woman that was
> on board all the while the ship lay in the country,
> being very Pox'd, which the dockter warranted
> sound on that terms Joyce Dudley took her, if not
> so by agreement was to pay for the cure.[8]

The diligent Francis Place, who collected all manner of social
records, preserved notes of many transactions involving the sale of
felons to American buyers. At Charleston, Carolina, in 1740 the
following account was made out:

> 17 convicts sold together
> @ £72 currency   = £1,224. 0. 0.
>
> *Charges:*
> Entry & certificate returned: £ 3.12. 0.
> Fresh meat & rice before landing: 17.10. 0.
> Lodgings till sold: 67. 0. 0.
> Commission @ 5%:   61. 0. 0.
>
>   £1,074.18.

In 1744 on the Potomac River eighty-four men and women convicts, all that remained of the 153 shipped from England, were sold for £211.10.0. sterling and 112,120 lbs of tobacco. At the same place a year later eighty-six convicts surviving from an original shipment of 125 were sold for £97.10.0. sterling and 117,452 lbs of tobacco. Place, having quoted other similar sales figures, provides the helpful information that, at this time, tobacco was valued at seven shillings sterling per hundredweight.[9] The trade in convicts was, therefore, showing a handsome profit, even allowing for the abnormally high shipboard death rate.[10]

When Andrew Reid succeeded Jonathan Forward[11] as Contractor for the Transports on 4 February 1742, the treatment of felons began rapidly to deteriorate. Even before his official duties began, Reid was in trouble. In September 1741 he received news that twenty-nine convicts he had shipped in the *Sally* for Virginia had "risen upon the ship's crew and carried her by force into the Texel." He had to call upon the Government for help, and they ordered the embattled convicts to be retaken, reshipped, or otherwise secured.[12]

The lawlessness of the 1740s also finds an echo in one of Reid's letters to the justices of Coventry of 8 September 1742 when he was arranging the delivery of a consignment of felons to his ship moored in the Thames:

> As I find by experience that carrying them to any of the Gaols about town, though but for a few days, is of great detriment to their healths, I beg I may be informed exactly where and about what hour they will arrive, that some body may attend to conduct them directly on board. It would be very agreeable as well as serviceable to me, and an act of great humanity to the prisoners and their fellow passengers, to have them shaved and their bodies as well as cloaths washed as clean as possible before they set out . . . Nothing contributes more to make a ship sickly than nastiness, which you may easily imagine has a very bad effect when one hundred unclean persons are cooped up between a ship's decks.[13]

For all his influence and notoriety, Andrew Reid remains a shadowy figure. He appears to have been Forward's agent in Port Tobacco, Maryland, before 1740 at much the same time as Jonathan Sydenham[14] was agent in Virginia. Both came to London upon Forward's retirement from business, Reid to succeed him as principal contractor for transportation from London and the Home Counties and Jonathan Sydenham as principal contractor for the other counties of England. In 1747 Reid was cited by Ralph Greene of London, the owner of the *Forward*, for failing to honour his agreement to victual and man that ship and to pay her crew during her last and ill-starred voyage in 1742. Greene estimated that Reid's profit from the sale of felons loaded in the ship would have been £1,700. She loaded tobacco in the Potomac River to freight to London but, off the Lizard, she was taken prize by a Spanish privateer from San Sebastian. Reid, defending this suit, pleaded that "transportation is always attended with very great risk and expense," and claimed that from several private contracts of sale of felons he had made only "£3 a head, or some such sum" (a palpably deflated figure); whereas he had needed "to make large provision of beef, pork, butter, cheese, bread, water casks, gin, clothes . . . and also of a surgeon, steward, cook and other servants, together with irons and chains, gratings, platforms and cabins . . . both for security and accommodation, and also an extraordinary number of seamen which are always necessary to prevent the felons rising upon them, whose wages are always very great by reason of the nature of such a cargo." Reid explained how felons had to be sold on credit to penurious planters, "by which means he [Reid] has long been out of his money, and some of the planters having since failed, he was likely to lose."[15] To support his hard luck story, Reid quoted from letters received from his agents. On 7 February 1744 Andrew Reid, Esq., wrote from Port Tobacco to explain the exceptionally long stay in port of Captain Sargent, Master of the *Forward*, due to

the embarrassment of his own affairs on Patuxent and by his carrying of his cargo of goods [i.e. felons] round the river to sell by retail while his ship lay in Potomack . . . Your servants by Captain Maxwell [of the *Indian Queen* which sailed from London in May 1743] sold indifferently well. I engaged Mr. Hamilton, the lawyer, to take Robinson [John Robinson, a felon reprieved for fourteen years' transportation] and allow him good wages, yet he choosed to stay at Scandalous House with a parcel of thieves. Pray what shall I do with Halley? She has cost me £14 already for clothes and board, and if I turn her about her business (for no body will buy a person of her violent passions) she will certainly come home. Indeed you desire me to keep her until you had seen her friends, but you are at the expense in the meantime.

I have never yet had time to go to the Eastern Shore to inquire into . . . the prices of servants in Chaptank but . . . I find they sell for 2000 to 2400 and sometimes 2700 [lbs of tobacco], but then it is light which they reprize with their store dealings and always allow 6% for cash . . . I imagine it would be best to keep to those three Rivers you are already engaged in than go upon uncertainties when the miscarriages will be attended with the consequences of the imputation of fecklessness and loss of fortune. I know you are fond of Patuxent but I am afraid there is scarce an opening. Potomack consignments on both sides of the river decline . . . Even the better sort wait till the height of the market and purchase their goods to send home for on commission . . . Your servants alone will never give your ship the necessary dispatch . . . and those who live 30 or 40 miles from [here] are obliged to trust to the honesty of 2 or 3 men to receive them . . . A cargo of servants can not be sold to any advantage without these inconveniencies.[16]

In 1747 Forward, no doubt repenting of his association with Andrew Reid because of the latter's unsavoury reputation, decided to make over to the firm of Sydenham and Hodgson (*see below*) rather than to Reid all his business interests in America including his agencies and trading networks.[17] By 1753, whether because he wished to retire to enjoy his wealth or because he was driven to it, Reid took into partnership a John Stewart who was designated to succeed him as contractor. In any event, Reid then withdrew to a more comfortable existence on his estate in South Carolina until his death in 1784.

Jonathan Sydenham, having taken into partnership a Thomas Hodgson, formerly clerk to Jonathan Forward, in order to begin trade as Sydenham and Hodgson, rose quickly to become one of the country's leading black slave dealers, in addition to securing contracts for the transportation of felons from English jails other than those in London and the Home Counties. This trade, based on Bristol and London, was supplemented by other merchandising ventures in the tobacco colonies. The enterprise was ill-starred. In 1756 the firm was sued by Samuel Foxworthy, owner of the *Mahon*, which Sydenham had chartered for a mercantile voyage to Maryland and which ran aground off Plymouth on her return voyage, for failing to pay either the agreed hire costs or the members of the crew. The ship was accordingly arrested by the High Court of Admiralty.[18] Hard on the heels of this suit came news of the death in Virginia of William Jordan in 1757. Jordan had been for many years Sydenham's principal agent in the colony and, even before his death, had become embroiled with his principal in a dispute over their financial transactions. After depositions had been taken in Virginia in 1762 to establish the extent of the debts of Sydenham and Hodgson,[19] the firm was declared bankrupt in the following year. This, however, did not deter Jonathan Forward Sydenham, who had become a partner in his father's business while still in his teens, from rebuilding the enterprise, now directed more intensively towards the trade in felons where profit went hand in hand with problems.

By 1768, and now able to describe himself as "the Contractor with the greatest part of the counties of England for the transportation of felons," it was Jonathan Forward Sydenham's turn to seek Government intervention to protect his interests. In August of that year a gang of cut-throat sailors had forced their way on board his ship, the *Middleton*, while it was lying at Limehouse Reach ready to embark a cargo of convicts, and demanded to be employed at wages of thirty-seven shillings a month, as against the prevailing rate of ten shillings, failing which they were ready to dismast the ship "and intimated their desire of turning the felons on shore."[20] An armed cutter was quickly despatched to the scene and the *Middleton* sailed without further incident.

Sydenham and Hodgson operated principally out of Bristol, then the premier port for emigration to the Americas, and employed their own sub-contractors. One of these, Samuel Sedgley, a prosperous slave trader and owner of a small fleet of ships which he used indifferently for white or black cargoes, with Jonathan Tallimay, captain of his fleet, became a familiar figure in Maryland harbours where he regularly discharged his transported felons. Sedgley did well enough at his trade to become Sheriff of Bristol in 1739 and built up the enterprise of Sedgley, Hilhouse and Randolph to conduct a mixed trade between Bristol and the American colonies, including the transportation of convicts from the western counties of England. Sedgley died in 1754 and the enterprise he founded outlived him for a few years before going bankrupt in 1767. In the following year the stepbrothers William Stevenson and James Cheston were carrying on the trade and took into partnership a substantial merchant named William Randolph. Their ships, including the *Randolph*, *William*, *Elizabeth* and *Isabella*, were regularly consigned to Messrs. Thomas and William Ringold of Kent County, Maryland.

In March 1763, after his long apprenticeship to the transportation business, John Stewart made a bid to become the first contractor with an exclusive nation-wide franchise. He wrote to the Treasury:

During the space of 16 years I have been so happy in the execution
of the Contract as never to have incurred the least censure or
question of my integrity. . . By Act of Parliament each County
or City was obliged to pay the charge of Transporting the Prisoners
therein ordered for Transportation. The City of London and County of Middlesex were most affected by this Law and therefore
made very early application to his Majesty for relief. The Courts
of Justice, having no authority to contract with any person for
Transporting Convicts . . . Contractors seldom offered, and the
Transports therefore remained in gaol till their numbers and other
effects of their situation brought fatal diseases amongst them,
especially in Newgate, whereby it became dangerous for the
King's Judges, and those who duty called to the Old Bailey, to
attend . . . The manner in which persons are transported from
those places that pay the expence of Transporting their own
Criminals does not come within my knowledge, but as they are
without the necessary rules of a Contract, in general it is attended
[to] by the Magistrates who, in the interior parts of the Kingdom,
are for the most part but ill qualified to judge of a maritime
affair so connected with commerce.[21]

For himself, Stewart claimed to have successfully interwoven his
business as a shipowner and merchant with his responsibility for the
transportation of criminals:

When your Lordships are pleased to consider that the Contractor,
in order to execute this part of Public Justice with any degree
of regularity which is indispensably necessary, must form his
mercantile business on a plan suitable thereto; that ships must be
provided for that end of a construction so far peculiar as to be
fit only for the Guinea [i.e. black slave] trade, whose burden is
given up to fast sailing and accommodations, and that correspon-
dencies abroad must be formed accordingly . . .[22]

He felt entitled to ask for a twenty-one-year contract. The Treasury,
not much impressed, signed for seven years without extending
Stewart's franchise beyond what it was previously.

During the last two decades of its lifespan the provisions of the
Transportation Act settled into a regular and efficient rhythm. When
John Stewart died in 1772 his place was taken by Duncan Campbell,
his former partner, who made a fortune from the export of convicts.
Much of his original correspondence relating to the conduct of his

transportation business survives, including the following letters to his
agents, Somervell & Noble and Hugh Lennox:

> London, 20th May 1773. This goes by the *Hanover Planter*, Capt.
> McCulloch, on board of which ship I have put 93 convicts
> consigned to Mr. Matthew Ridley in Baltimore Town in Maryland
> and have agreed to give for freight, as per Bill of Lading, 30s.
> per head upon 93 people, amounting to £139.10s., for which I
> shall credit the account of Messrs. Somervell & Noble, and you
> will settle that business amongst yourselves accordingly. By the
> account inclosed, which I send for your Government, you will
> see what moneys have been paid to the Captain and others on
> account of your ship. As you have been put to little or no
> additional expence on account of my servants in the outfit of the
> vessel . . . the freight will be nearly all clear gain and help to
> make up for the misfortunes in the former part of her voyage. I
> have desired my agent to take the servants away as expeditiously
> as possible that the Captain may the sooner be able to follow
> your instructions for his future proceedings . . .

> London, 4th November 1773 via the *New York Packet*. I have
> had many pieces of business to transact but I own this [the
> *Hanover Packet*] was the most troublesome. The Jews [probably
> including Abraham Moses Fernandez and Moses Israel Fonseca],
> who were the freighters, were of the lower class and gave me
> infinite trouble, some of which I was obliged to sue, others to
> leave their disputes to arbitration. This, added to an inexperienced
> and indistinct Captain, made matters worse . . . It gave me great
> satisfaction to find McCulloch delivered his servants in good
> order. I have some notion he would make me a good Captain. I
> should like such a man when he is a little civilized; he seems
> very industrious.[23]

When, in 1779, Campbell was examined by a House of Commons
committee, he reported that he had transported criminals for twenty
years at the rate of £5 a head, except in the last three years of the
business when, because of competition for the business, he had agreed
to take felons "without any profit but that which accrued to him by
disposing of their servitude in the Colonies." Many of the convicts
who had money had "bought off their servitude, and their punishment
was only banishment." He had carried felons only to Maryland and
Virginia where he sold "common male convicts not artificers on
average for £10 each, females at £8 to £9, and tradesmen for £15
to £25 . . . The old and infirm he used to dispose of to those humane

People who chose to take them, but with some he was obliged to give Premiums." He believed (and the American "rebellion" was in its fifth year) that convicts could not be disposed of in colonies other than Maryland and Virginia though Georgia might be persuaded to take 100 a year. Campbell reckoned that over a seven-year period he had transported 473 convicts a year, carrying between 100 and 200 persons in one ship. The normal time for the transatlantic crossing was two months but the convicts used often to remain in jail for the same length of time awaiting a ship to carry them. During his period of office he estimated that rather more than one in seven of the convicted felons had died before reaching America, "many of gaol fever, but more of smallpox; but twice as many men as women died."[24]

Until the last gasp of the official transportation scheme to colonial America, private enterprise apparently kept up a parallel supply of kidnapped labourers. In June 1775 Elizabeth Brickleband, then aged seventeen, was lured from her home in London by a woman who operated as a talent scout for "professional" shipping agents John and Jane Dennison. Within days Elizabeth was carried on board the ship Nancy with about a hundred other "indentured servants" and despatched to America for a term of twenty-one years. When her mother threatened to prosecute the Dennisons, they first tried threats and then bribery but to no avail. At their trial in April 1776, evidence was given that Henry Quiforth, as agent for the *Nancy*, had received £9.7s.6d. for acquiring the hundred passengers and that the appearance of Elizabeth Brickleband's name on the passenger list "was the only indenture she ever had." The Dennisons received sentence of three months' imprisonment each but what became of Elizabeth Brickleband was not disclosed at the trial.[25]

NOTES

1. PRO (Public Record Office): Privy Council Unbound Papers, 1/46-57.

2. PRO: Chancery suit, C11/1902/11.

3. *Ibid.*, C11/1984/23.

4. Darby Lux made his last voyage as a ship's captain in 1738, then settled in Maryland as Jonathan Forward's principal agent.

5. PRO: Treasury Papers, T1/409. At least one of the transported felons, Jane Bailey, appears, however, to have been shipped originally by the *Hercules* before being taken into Vigo by the French (SP 44/88/28).

6. PRO: Chancery suit, C11/260/69.

7. *Ibid.*, C11/1223/28 and C11/685/3.

8. *Ibid.*, C11/1851/26.

9. British Library Add. Mss. 27,826. Francis Place assembled no fewer than seventy-one volumes of material.

10. Convict labour tended to be substantially cheaper than that of black slaves: the services of a healthy young felon over a period of seven years could be purchased for £12-15 sterling while a black slave might cost £50 sterling.

11. Jonathan Forward died at the age of eighty in 1760, wealthy and unmourned. By his will he left much of his property to his grandson Edward Stephenson, including a share of the Iron Gate Wharf by St. Katherine's. His extensive estates in the West Country were bequeathed to his daughter Elizabeth, wife of Robert Byng, seventh son of Viscount Torrington. On her marriage in 1734 she was worth an estimated £10,000. Robert Byng became Paymaster of the Navy and then Governor of Barbados. His son Robert Byng was one of those smothered in the Black Hole of Calcutta in 1756.

12. Historical Manuscripts Commission: *Fourteenth Report*, Appendix 9 (Earl of Buckingham MSS), p. 77.

13. Coventry City Records of Transportation.

14. PRO: London Depositions in Chancery, C24/1588/26. Jonathan Sydenham the elder married Mary, daughter of John Morton of Richmond, Virginia, and half-sister of John Morton Jordan of Annapolis, Maryland, agent for Lord Baltimore. Sydenham became a justice of the peace and coroner for King George County, Virginia.

15. PRO: Chancery suit, C11/2499/19.

16. *Ibid.*

17. British Library Add. Charters 26400 and 26404 by which Jonathan Forward, tobacco merchant of London, assigned his business debts in Virginia and Maryland to John Goodwin of London, and his trade in Virginia to Jonathan Sydenham and Thomas Hodgson.

18. PRO: Chancery suit, C11/1120/9 and C11/1124/9.

19. PRO: Depositions in *Jonathan Sydenham & Thomas Hodgson* v. *John Morton Jordan*, C12/882/16.

20. PRO: State Papers Criminal, SP 44/232/40.

21. PRO: Treasury Papers, T1/416.

22. *Ibid.*

23. This correspondence is taken from the letter books of Duncan Campbell, which begin with the death of his partner John Stewart on 18 February 1772. They offer a fascinating insight not only into his family life, shipping and property speculations, but into the day-to-day administration of his transportation activities. The letter books are in the custody of the Mitchell Library, Macquaire Street, Sydney, Australia.

24. *House of Commons Journal*, 37:310 ff.

25. Old Bailey Sessions Papers for April 1776.

CHAPTER VII

The Scottish Experiment

Scotland, always tenacious in preserving its own laws and customs despite the Act of Union of 1707 [uniting England and Scotland into one Kingdom], came late to the practice of criminal transportation as a by-product of the legal system. Some procrastination in this regard may be better understood following the wholesale deportation of thousands of young Scots, amongst the flower of the country, after the uprisings of 1715 and 1745. It was not until 1766 that Scotland adopted the English practice of deporting its criminal elements to America and began to appoint its own contractors for the purpose,[1] but, from long before that time, local enterprise and initiative had contrived to ensure a regular supply of youthful labour to the colonies. It was not only the merchants of Bristol who were able to run a brisk and profitable trade in servile labour by rounding up innocent youths and shipping them off to be sold to plantation owners. The dark practices of press gangs, indentured servitude and felon transportation, which were backed by the full might of the law, could with great ease shade off into coercion and then to kidnapping, provided always that the victims were of the common sort and not liable to know of or strive for their legal rights. Once human labour had become a saleable commodity in the sugar and tobacco plantations, the enterprise of merchant adventurers could be relied upon to satisfy the laws of supply and demand. Their talent was the more necessary in Scotland before the realisation dawned that such labour could be even more cheaply provided by a regular venting of the prisons.

Apart from the flurry of reforming zeal shown by the Parliament in the 1650s, the scandal of organised child snatching in furtherance of mercantile ends appears to have escaped public attention until late in the 1700s, and then not because of the concern or vigilance of any liberal institution or State authority, but through a singularly

tough and resourceful Scotsman, Peter Williamson, who had himself
been the victim of a kidnap. It is to him that we owe an accurate
and detailed account of the nature and scale of this sordid trade as
it was plied in only one of Britain's seaports.[2]

Williamson was one of the many children of a poor but respectable
crofter of Aboyne in Aberdeenshire who, when his mother died in
his eighth year, was packed off to Aberdeen to be cared for by an
aunt. One day, while he was playing on a quayside, he was approached
by two men from a nearby ship who lured him away with the promise
of a new life of ease and plenty. He later discovered that these two
men were recruitment agents for a local saddler, James Smith, one
of fifteen merchants of Aberdeen who at that time were directing
their skills to decoying footloose youths into plantation service
overseas in unholy alliance with the city's justices. Each of these
merchants employed gangs to discover and procure new sources of
labour either by false promises or, if necessary, by force. Some even
sent out their hirelings on horseback to scour the surrounding
countryside. Their combined efforts provided full shiploads of sixty
boys and girls at a time who were paraded before the local justices
to undergo a parody of indenturing. In the troubled 1740s a common
sight in Aberdeen was a flock of local lads and lassies, mixed in
with strapping youths from the Highlands, being driven with staves
and horse whips along the main thoroughfares under the superinten-
dence of drovers to an assembly point to await loading on the next
ship to America. Those who proved recalcitrant or who threatened
to escape were locked up in the city prison or workhouse. During
their brief wait on shore, the captives were provisioned at the rate
of twenty pence a week each by one Helen Law whose own son had
been seized and transported to the plantations in the same way. When
Peter Williamson himself was similarly confined, his father came into
town to look for him but discovered that he was powerless to act
since the law and local custom obliged parents to reimburse the
merchants for every last penny they claimed to have spent on the
children. Many local parents could tell agonising tales of forced
separations and it became customary for well-meaning townsfolk to
visit the places where the children were confined in order to take
note of who they were and to give their families some account of
them.

Almost all the inhabitants of Aberdeen . . . knew the traffick . . . which was carried on in the market places, in the High Street, and in the avenues to the town in the most public manner . . . The trade in carrying off boys to the plantations in America and selling them there as slaves was carried on with an amazing effrontery . . . and by open violence. The whole neighbouring country were alarmed at it. They would not allow their children to go to Aberdeen for fear of being kidnapped. When they kept them at home, emissaries were sent out by the merchants who took them by violence from their parents [and] if a child was amissing, it was immediately suspected that he was kidnapped by the Aberdeen merchants.

In July 1743, with sixty-nine other youngsters, Peter Williamson was put on board Captain Robert Bragg's ship, the *Planter*, bound for Virginia:

They conducted me between the decks to some others they had kidnapped [but] I had no sense of the fate that was destined for me and spent the time in childish amusements with my fellow sufferers in the steerage, being never suffered to go up on deck while the vessel was in harbour, which was until such a time as they had got in their loading with a complement of unhappy youths for carrying on their wretched commerce. The treatment we met with . . . I hope I may be excused from relating. We struck a sand bank near the Capes of Delaware but bailed out and the crew left us to perish. We were taken on shore to a sort of camp and then taken on a vessel bound to Philadelphia. The original vessel was entirely lost. When we arrived and landed at Philadelphia, that Captain soon had people enough who came to buy us. He made the most of his villainous loading after his disaster and sold us at about £16 a head. What became of my unhappy companions I never knew.

The fate of some few of Williamson's compatriots, however, emerged from subsequent examination of witnesses. A George Johnson, sent by his uncle to Virginia to be placed under the care of a friend there, travelled in Captain Ferguson's ship, the *Indian Queen*, with sixty other boys, many of whom had been taken from their families without their parents' consent. Two brothers on the same ship, James and William Sheds, aged fifteen and six, were sold to John Graham in Quantigo Creek, Virginia, and when James ran away, he was whipped severely and ordered to serve another year for his desertion. According to Johnson, most of such boys were very harshly used during their time of service and were often forced to desperate measures to get away. At the end of his indentured time, each boy received fifty shillings, but nothing else by way of encouragement. John Ingram and his wife sent their son James, when he was twelve years old, on an errand into Aberdeen where he was seized by the agents of merchant Alexander Gray and taken without consent to the plantations. He was never heard of again.

A similar story was told by William Jamieson of his son John who went missing from his home at Old Meldrum in 1741 when he was aged eleven. When he was reported to have been taken up by merchant "Bonny" John Burnet for shipment to the colonies, William Jamieson was advised that he would not obtain redress from the local magistrates since they all had a hand in the affair. However, when he learned that his son had been shipped to Maryland, he procured a warrant in Edinburgh which allowed him to proceed against Burnet, only to find that no court official in Aberdeen would deliver the warrant. Jamieson finally sought the aid of his landlord, the Earl of Aberdeen, and Burnet was at last overawed into promising the son's return within twelve months. Unhappily the Earl then died, Burnet went bankrupt and fled the country, and John Jamieson was left as yet another name on the list of those who disappeared from their homeland in the cause of profit. As Peter Williamson commented:

> The subject is calculated to open the eyes of the deluded poor, many of whom have suffered tribulation for the loss of their children. It is absurd to imagine that any parent, tho' in ever so necessitous a condition, would dispose of their own flesh and blood to strangers who make a prey of innocent children to accumulate their ill-gotten wealth and support their grandeur by conveying the unhappy victims to the remotest parts of the globe where they can have no redress for the injuries done them.

Once in Philadelphia, Peter Williamson was sold for seven years to another Scotsman, Hugh Wilson, who had himself been kidnapped as a young man from his home in Perth. Wilson was,

> contrary to many others of his calling, a humane, worthy, honest man. Having no children of his own, and commiserating with my unhappy condition, he took great care of me until I was fit for business, and about the twelfth year of my age set me about little trifles in which I continued until my fourteenth year when I was

more fit for harder work. He agreed to send me to school every winter for five years. I continued with him until I was 17 when he died leaving me £200 currency [then worth £120 sterling], his best horse and a saddle. I went jobbing about the country for nearly seven years. I applied for marriage to the daughter of a substantial planter and, on being found acceptable, we were married. My father-in-law gave me land on the frontier in Berks Co. near the forks of the Delaware of 200 acres. I settled there and was happy in a good wife. In 1754 the French Indians became troublesome and committed daily savageries. My wife went to visit some relations and at 11 p.m. I heard the savages' war cry. They tried to get in and I threatened them with a loaded gun. They threatened to burn me alive if I did not come out. They rushed me, disarmed me, bound me to a tree and plundered and destroyed everything and burned the whole. I was threatened by a tomahawk to be killed if I did not go with them, was loaded with a great pack and travelled at night. At daybreak they tied me to a tree and forced blood out of my fingernails and then lit a fire near the tree and danced around me. They found a way into the house of Jacob Snider, his wife, five children and a servant. They scalped the parents and children and took a young man but, because he complained, he was also scalped and killed. They then scalped John Adams' wife and four children before his eyes and took the old man off, sometimes stripping him naked and painting him or plucking hairs from his head [and] scorched his cheeks with hot coals.

After describing other atrocities carried out by the Indians, Williamson relates how he at last escaped to reach his father-in-law's house in Chester County only to find that his wife had died two months previously. He joined the Army for three years and "took revenge on the Indians by scalping them." On his discharge in Plymouth, England, in 1757 he put to good account all that he and many others like him had suffered. He began a single-handed crusade to bring to public notice the evils of the illicit trade in children and, within a year of his return, had published a volume, shrewdly calculated by its title to appeal to a wide readership.[3] This book, published in York, spoke plainly of foul practices in Aberdeen and did not hesitate to name names, for which reason the magistracy of Aberdeen condemned it as libellous. The author was summoned to appear before the Aberdeen bench, was found guilty of libel, fined ten shillings and thrown into jail, while his book was ordered to be publicly burned. Williamson commented sardonically: "He must have been a very youthful magistrate in 1758 who could not remember some circumstances of a public branch of trade carried out in 1744." Not content to submit to such a parody of justice, Williamson now prepared a prosecution against his detractors to be heard in the Court of Session in Edinburgh. Meanwhile his book, its circulation now boosted by the notoriety it had achieved, ran into several editions, and honest witnesses had been assembled who would substantiate every accusation made in it.

Called to account for their undoubted complicity in the trade, the Aberdeen magistrates succeeded in blackening the case against them by the defence they submitted. They were obliged to concede that the kidnapping of children had taken place on a large scale but claimed, against solid evidence to the contrary, that no children under the age of ten had ever been indentured except by their parents' consent, and never shipped off if they were claimed by their parents or friends. Overtaken by sanctimonious resentment, one of the defendants went so far as to claim that what he had done amounted to a public service performed out of charity since many of those he indentured as plantation servants were taken "when provisions were scarce [and] had been turned away by their Masters who could not afford them bread." The benefactor in this case was one George Garloch who, while unable to call to mind the names of any who had thus benefited from his munificence, remembered that each servant sold in America had fetched a price of between £5 and £8. But the very next defence witness, an Aberdeen shipowner, remembered the price as being £10 a head.

The Court of Session, unimpressed by the defendants' display of honour and virtue, found them liable to pay £100 damages and expenses to Williamson, "the same to be no burden on the town of Aberdeen," and ordered the town's account books to remain in court. Two former bailees of Aberdeen who had regarded Williamson's pamphlets as an undeserved reproach on the merchants of Aberdeen, and Williamson himself as an idle stroller who could give no good account of himself, wrote indignantly to the court:

> We are sorry to find . . . that there is a sentence pronounced against us in Williamson's process whereby we are deemed to pay to him a very large sum out of our private pockets. We think it necessary to inform you that our conduct and intentions, with regard to our sentence against him, have been entirely misunderstood. We can with the greatest integrity declare that .

. . neither of us knew, directly or indirectly, that Walter Cochran, the depute clerk, was in any ways concerned in transporting boys to America, nor that there ever was in being the book he produced in the proof; that neither of us had never any interest or concern in such trade; that we never knew, and did not believe, that any men and boys were ever transported from Aberdeen to America contrary to law . . . You will easily perceive . . . how hard a thing it is to be decerned to pay a sum of money, as a fine, for doing what we considered to be our duty.[4]

Williamson's experience of the American plantations was both formative and haunting. Upon it he based his counsel to a rising generation of potential emigrants:

The planters will buy, some ten and others twenty, to labour in their plantations and cultivate their ground. Thus we were driven through the country like cattle to a Smithfield [i.e. butchers'] market and exposed to sale in public fairs as so many brute beasts. If the devil had come in the shape of a man to purchase us, his money would have been as readily accepted as of the honestest and most humane man in the world. These children are sometimes sold to barbarous and cruel masters from whom they often make an elopement to avoid the harsh usage they often meet with, but as there is scarce a possibility of making a total escape, they are generally taken and brought back; and for every day they have been absent they are compelled to serve a week, for every week a month, and for every month a year.[5] They are besides obliged to pay the cost of advertising and bringing them back which often protracts their slavery four or five times longer. Some of these poor deluded slaves, in order to put an end to their bondage, put a period to their lives.

The planters themselves are generally of an idle, indolent disposition, not caring to fatigue themselves with work. How soon, therefore, they can raise £20 or £30 they purchase servants from the European merchants whom they make slaves. These they send to the woods or employ them in other kinds of hard labour. If they fail to perform a certain task in a day they are severely punished by their masters who review their work at night. Nor dare the servant, when he is thus chastised, presume to vindicate himself for fear of giving new offence to this unrelenting tyrant whose humour must be indulged even at the expense of strokes and blows. This is more especially the case in Maryland and Virginia. These two are the best markets to which our European merchants can resort for the sale of their illicit cargoes of slaves.

Here they may barter them for tobacco upon which they have an immense return of profit.

The servants in Maryland are mostly convicts yet some of them, when their period of slavery is over, acquire plantations of their own and are very expert in raising tobacco. They frequently contract with their correspondents in Europe to send them over men, women and children to be employed. But their promises are so pernicious to those they engage that they generally prove their utter destruction. They intice those ignorant creatures to believe they are to have high wages payable in their mother country, but they will find it quite the contrary. You who indent yourselves in this manner labour under another disadvantage. In that country they have the natural presumption that when men and women agree to transport themselves as slaves, they must have been guilty of some notorious crime; they are looked upon as in the black class of convicts. For some time honest people who had engaged to serve suffered considerably on this account as these renegadoes were allowed to be evidences against them and to swear away their reputations.

You will perhaps be told you are going to a country flowing with milk and honey. These, it is true, are to be had in great plenty in America, but before you come to enjoy them you will find that you must work through an ocean of labour and fatigue. Whereas, if you are possessed of but £3 or £4 to pay your passage and are of an ingenious disposition, you are certain not only of handsome bread but, by modest frugality and industry, of making a genteel fortune in a few years.

By 1772 the Government had become thoroughly alarmed at reports of a tidal wave of emigration to America, particularly from Scotland, and decreed that each major port in the British Isles was to submit returns of all those embarking for foreign ports, showing their names, ages, occupations and reasons for leaving. (The rather slipshod drafting of this order caused fury amongst many well-to-do citizens who found themselves subjected to cross-examination when they set off on excursions to Europe.) At the same time Whitehall appointed the Lord Justice Clark of Scotland to make more careful enquiry about the causes and extent of emigration from those parts.

No sooner had he begun his investigations than he questioned why the Government itself was sanctioning the transportation of convicts. He wrote in October 1773: "I think it is to be regretted that the law, as it stands at present, does not admit of a greater diversity of punishments according to the different nature of crimes and circumstances of the offender. In this part of the kingdom transportation to America begins to lack every characteristic of punishment." It was clearly the hardship of conditions at home compared with the descriptions of life in the New World that was spurring an exodus he feared would become "epidemical."

He discovered, when twelve people were tried in Glasgow for joining an unlawful combination of journeymen weavers in Paisley, that the members of the combination had been reduced to such beggary that they threatened to embark for America in one body. He described as "a dangerous situation" the enticements of Canadian and American landlords who provided their own ships to take willing emigrants for as little as a guinea a head. These reports and the returns from port officials together made it "appear to His Majesty that the emigrations are very detrimental to the general good of the State, and every proper check within the power of Government should be given to plans which tend so fatally to depopulate a considerable part of his Kingdoms."[6]

NOTES

1. In 1772 the official contractor was a merchant of Glasgow named Patrick Colquhoun, so one learns from Home Office papers which note that two Scotsmen were pardoned for house-breaking on condition that they served with Colquhoun.

2. Peter Williamson, *Life and Adventures*. The most complete version, to which is added the evidence of witnesses to the events of the 1740s, was published in Aberdeen in 1757. Editions continued to appear until the mid-nineteenth century, some with portraits of the author dressed as a Delaware Indian.

3. This carried a long and perhaps intentionally obscure title beginning *Some Considerations on the Current State of Affairs* . . . and was published in York in 1758. A roughly contemporary volume, published in Glasgow and designed for less refined tastes, appeared under the title of *French and Indian Cruelty Exemplified*.

4. Peter Williamson, *op. cit.* (Aberdeen, 1801), p. 138.

5. *Cf.* James Revel's account in chapter VIII.

6. *Calendar of Home Office Papers 1773-1775* (London, 1899), Nos. 324 and 331.

CHAPTER VIII

His Majesty's Seven-Year Passengers

Only a minority of those transported for their crimes could be counted as literate, and those few were seldom inspired to leave to posterity an account of their lives or of their voyage to the New World as "His Majesty's Seven-Year Passengers," the term by which such emigrants were known colloquially. Merchants and ships' officers engaged in the transportation trade, for quite different reasons, left behind them scant records of their enterprises. One is left to conjecture about the cost in human misery of a normal transatlantic crossing from those few calculations made in recent years suggesting that, in the period from 1620 to 1680, some 35 percent of women and 50 percent of men sent to the Americas as indentured servants died on shipboard. While this figure may well be exaggerated, it does suggest that the risks to be expected from a long sea voyage were enough to discourage all but the hardiest and healthiest from undertaking it. The only statistical study so far carried out into the shipboard mortality rate amongst transported felons concludes that throughout the period 1718 to 1736 the death rate was 14 percent, a figure which had hardly changed by the late 1770s.[1] These statistics provide a sobering antidote to some of the more inflated estimates which have appeared in print.[2] It is unreasonable to assume that convicts were at conspicuously greater peril than paying passengers, and in some respects they might almost be said to have been better cared for. While gross brutality was known to be exercised against some convicts on passage, ranging from summary execution to regular beatings,[3] it was to be reckoned a rarity since they were a saleable commodity, priced according to their condition on arrival.[4] Moreover, since the Transportation Act of 1718, all the ships regularly engaged in freighting convicts carried a surgeon, and many captains took a share in the profits from the sale of their passengers. Against these factors it has to be recognised that many of the transported felons were elderly or infirm, unlikely to fetch a good price and therefore dispensable; jail fever racked the transport ships every year; and the convicts were stowed in overcrowded and insanitary conditions even when they were not shackled in leg irons and manacles.

One of the few surviving first-hand accounts of what shipboard life meant for those beginning their term of transportation comes from the pens of Marcellus Rivers and Oxenbridge Foyle. These two were taken prisoner in 1655 on suspicion of having been involved in the irresolute uprising in Salisbury, Wiltshire, which was fiercely suppressed. Many concealed themselves until they could flee overseas. On Cromwell's orders, the judges proceeded with the utmost severity against the rest so that many were executed and others sent as slaves to Barbados where they received such harsh treatment that few ever returned home. Rivers and Foyle, without trial or examination, were taken to Plymouth with others, including common felons, and put aboard the *John* of London, under Captain John Cole, to be transported and sold. Both men survived to return to England and to write a pamphlet on behalf of themselves and seventy other Englishmen who were sold into slavery with them. To this book they gave the title *England's Slavery or Barbados Merchandize*[5] and prefaced it with a most fitting quotation from the Book of Exodus: "And God spake all these words, saying, 'He that stealeth a man and selleth him, or if he be found in his hand, he shall surely be put to death.'" During their five weeks' passage to Barbados they were

> all the way kept under decks and guards amongst horses [so] that their souls through heat and steam under the Tropick fainted in them, and never till they came to the Island knew whether [whither] they were going. . . We were all put under deck together and lockt down. On the same deck was a bulk-head, through which were port-holes made, and through them great guns laden with case-shot levelled against us so, if there should have been any rebellion under that tyranny . . . then might the Guard and Gunners more easily destroy us . . . Whereas every vitious servant which Bridewell and Newgate had vomited into that ship had a Hamaka to sleep in and keep him from the vermin, which amongst such a crew must inevitably swarm all the voyage untill the Extremity of heat destroy them, we were forced to ly on the bare hard boards, they refusing to let us have so much as mattes to ease our weary bones.

A similarly distressing tale was told some years later by John Coad who took part in Monmouth's Rebellion in 1685, was wounded and captured, sentenced at Wells Assizes, taken to Weymouth and put aboard a ship bound for Jamaica to be sold into slavery.

> The master of the ship shut 99 of us under deck in a very small room where we could not lay ourselves down without lying one upon another. The hatchway being guarded with a continual watch with blunderbusses and hangers, we were not suffered to go above deck for air or easement, but a vessel was set in the midst to receive the excrement, by which means the ship was soon infected with grievous and contagious diseases as the smallpox, fever, calenture and the plague with frightful botches. Of each of these diseases several died, for we lost of our company 22 men. This was the straitest prison that I was ever in, full of crying and dying, from whence there can be no flying . . . We had enough in the day to behold the miserable sight of botches, pox, others devoured with lice till they were almost at death's dore. In the night fearful cries and groning of sick and distracted persons which could not rest but lay tumbling over the rest . . . [The free passengers] would bestow upon us some part of their provision in secret to help satisfie our hunger for the wicked wretch [the master] would not allow no provision though there was enough in the ship and to spare. Some days we had not enough in five men's mess to suffice one man for one meal. . . Our water was also exceeding corrupt and stinking, and also very scarce to be had.[6]

Even in times of great difficulty, the State took pains to ensure that those to be deported, including felons under sentence of transportation, were removed from the kingdom as promptly as ships became available, and any long delays could be counted upon to provoke hostile reaction. A ship under embargo on the Thames in 1665 aroused so much concern that a petition was got up to have her moved "because her freight outward was solely forty passengers [convicts], but rather destructive in their idle course of life, whereunto they would most willingly return upon any advantage given to them for escape." In January 1740, at the height of the war with France and Spain when most ships were embargoed, the *York*, under Samuel Dickenson, with 100 felons from Newgate on board, was accorded a protected passage to the plantations.[7]

Convicts and indentured servants frequently shared the same ship, though quartered separately. "The ship began now to fill," says Moll Flanders, "several passengers came on board who were embarked on no criminal account, and these had accommodation assigned to them in the Great Cabin and other parts of the ship, whereas we, as convicts, were thrust down below, I know not where. . . . Some ordinary passengers [were] quartered in the steerage, and . . . our old fraternity were kept under the hatches . . . and came very little on deck. We [the convicts] were . . . kept so close I thought I should have been suffocated . . ."[8]

Little had changed in half a century and more when James Revel penned his doggerel ode, *The Poor Unhappy Transported Felons Sorrowful Account of Fourteen Years' Transportation at Virginia in America*.[9] Revel was convicted at the Surrey Assizes in 1771 and sentenced to be transported for fourteen years. Having lodged an appeal, he was taken from the transportation ship to be heard, but his sentence was confirmed and he was deported to Virginia in April 1771 by the ship *Thornton*. In his role as anti-hero Revel, as he embarks to begin his sentence, intones:

> I'd rather chuse to die than go.
> In vain I grieved, in vain my parents wept,
> For I was quickly sent on board the ship.

> With melting kisses and a heavy heart,
> I from my dearest parents then did part.
> In a few days we left the river quite
> And in short time of land we lost the sight.

> The Captain and the sailors us'd us well,
> But kept us nude lest we should rebel.
> We were in number about three score,
> A wicked lousy crew as e'er went o'er.

> Oaths and tobacco with us plenty were,
> For most did smoak and all did curse and swear.
> Five of our number in the passage died,
> Which soon was thrown into the ocean wide.

> And after sailing seven weeks or more,
> We at Virginia all were set on shore
> Where to refresh us we were washed clean,
> That to our buyers we might better seem.

> Our things they gave to each they did belong,
> And they that had clean linen put it on.

They shav'd our faces, comb'd our wigs and hair,
That we in decent order might appear.

Against the planters did come down to view
How well they lik'd this fresh transported crew.
The women from us separated stood
As well as us by them for to be viewed.

The indefatigable Mr. Place collected details of how the convict ships were provisioned for the voyage to America and itemises what was shipped for the use of 138 felons and a ship's company of twenty men:[10]

5 bushels of salt	2 oz. nutmeg
½ firkin soft soap	12 lbs. brimstone
40 lbs. ordinary tobacco	1 cask of vinegar
5 tons small beer for ship's co.	30 mess bowls
4 chaldrons of coal	13 doz. spoons
1 cwt. cheese	4 iron-bound tubs
4 lbs. pepper	1 gall. of oil
4 lbs. mustard	480 candles
8 lbs. rice	48 lbs. binnacle candles

For each mess of six men and boys there was provided each week, according to Place, 34 lbs. of bread, 19 lbs. of beef, 11 lbs. of pork, 7 lbs. of flour, 2 lbs. of suet, 5 gills of brandy, 134 quarts of water, and 4 quarts of pease: from this he conjectured that each convict received 1 lb. and 4 oz. of food per day. The weekly diet sheets for each six-man mess were supposedly:

Sunday: 4 lbs. of bread, 3 lbs. of pork, 1½ qts. of
           pease, and 18 quarts of water.

Monday: 4 lbs. of bread, 2 qts. of oatmeal, 1½ ozs.
           molasses, 1 lb. cheese, 18 quarts of water.

Tuesday }   4 lbs. of bread, 4 lbs. of beef,

Wednesday}: 1½ qts. of pease,

Thursday }   18 quarts of water.

Friday: 4 lbs. of bread, 2 qts. of oatmeal, 1½ ozs. of
                 molasses, 1 lb. of cheese, 18 quarts of
                 water.

Saturday: 4 lbs. of bread, 2 qts. of oatmeal, 3 gills of
                 Geneva at night.

Treatment of convicts on board ship was capable of veering from
one extreme of liberality to another of brutality depending upon the
nature and expectation of the officers. "Wild management" was by
no means exceptional. Jonathan Forward's agent in Virginia wrote
to his principal in 1725 to complain of the behaviour of the captain
and supercargo of the *Forward*:

> . . . for instead of their restraining the people from drinking, they
> gave them all the encouragement to drink and to be common
> drunk as they too often was . . . I did not believe at the first
> that it was possible that they could be so extravagant: but when
> Master and Merchant keep each of them a Mistress in their cabin
> coming over from England to Virginia, I must believe that it
> occasions great embezlement in provisions; and where there is
> such governors in a ship, the owner of such a cargo must be a
> great sufferer, for when they came to their anchoring at Vailers
> Hole they had not so much as a barrel of beef left, nor none of
> the Servants' provisions. I must believe that you provisioned the
> ship better out than that, but if she had as much more provisions
> from London it would have been all one . . . And as for the
> accident in the ship, it may be purely laid to the careless fellow
> Brockett and the carpenter and the Mate for their neglect in
> sounding the pump.[11]

To judge from the number of disputes which arose on the subject,
and from the testimony of expert witnesses (to which reference will
be made later), the ships regularly used for transportation were barely
fit for the purpose, though the flagships of the fleet, pompously
christened the *Tryal* and the *Justitia*, were probably exceptions.[12] The
constant risk of shipwreck and the heavy cost of repairs to many of
the rotting hulks in use were not the least of the contractors' worries
and it is remarkable how few convict ships were lost on the transatlantic run. One example will suffice. In November 1740 the executors of Margaret Johnson of Wapping, owner of the former convict
ship *Loyal Margaret*, sued Jonathan Forward to recover charter fees
of £350 for the ship's voyage from the West Indies with a cargo of

tobacco, sugar and rum. They were informed that only £56 was payable, the rest of the money having been spent on repairs just to keep the ship afloat.[13]

Matters went from bad to worse under Andrew Reid. John Sargent wrote to him from the *Forward* in Potomac River in December 1742:

> Arrived safe after my long, dismal passage of 8 weeks 4 days . . . Your fellons is likely to come to a good market. I have been with Cornel Presly to deliver the horse in good order. I should a made the passage in five weeks but myself and all my men could not come upon deck, the ship drivine up an down the sea, and not one man to direct them. Such a dismal sight I never saw before. The dockter and boy held it brave . . . The dockter, two days before we made the land, was taken with the same distemper and is now on shore in a dangerous way, which I am very sorry for, for may coully say as don as much as any man possable could do for your interest.

Having then recorded his complaints about the wretched state of his ship, Sargent added,

> I did expect either to be killed by the fellons every day, or the ship to sink; but they never offered nothing, and all the damage they did was in [the] hould in drinking out all the bear and wine they could get at . . . We now have living 107 as brave, comely fellows as ever was brought into Maryland and Virginia.

Since he had set out with 190 felons aboard his ship, Sargent was constrained to put the best face on things, and to console Reid for the loss of forty men and forty-three women he observed that twenty-five of the dead were "old men not worth £25."[14]

Andrew Reid's first recourse was against the owner of the ship, to whom he complained that the felons on board had died mainly, if not solely, because the vessel was badly fitted out so that

> both sea and rain were unavoidably lett in upon the felons thro' the ship's upper works, and that soon after their arrival several more of them died which was owing likewise to their having catched colds and other distempers . . . The rest were in so bad a condition . . . that only 87 of them were sold by July 1743 . . . for only £145 sterling (£241 Virginia currency), most on credit to the tobacco planters.

Reid then plotted his revenge both on John Sargent and on another of his more notorious captains, Barnet Bond of the *Justitia*, for their incompetence and carelessness. In March 1744 he acquainted the Admiralty that they had "been guilty of murther and felonies on the high seas."[15] After a preliminary enquiry, a warrant was issued for the committal of Sargent and Bond until their trial could take place before a special court of Oyer and Terminer "in regard of the heinousness of the facts and the difficulty of keeping the evidence [witnesses] together, who are seafaring men." Nothing abashed, Reid sought to have the trial conducted at the public expense, but the Admiralty were quick to reject the suggestion. On 24 March 1744 crew members of both convict ships were examined under oath.[16]

James Corrie of St. Martin's-le-Grand, London, aged twenty-six, chief mate of the *Justitia*, deposed that the ship took on board 163 felons and servants, some at Rotherhithe, others near the Red House at Deptford, and the last contingent at Gravesend. On Captain Bond's order, all the felons were searched as they came aboard, and all their money, knives and razors confiscated for the security of the ship and to prevent any attempt at escape. Despite this, several felons contrived to get free of their irons before the *Justitia* left the Thames and they were ordered up on deck again, one at a time, to be searched once more. Bond personally searched one felon, Nicholas Catt, who was found to have more than two guineas secreted away. When the ship finally sailed on 23 March 1743, she was carrying forty-two casks of water, each containing 180 gallons, and forty casks of 120 gallons each, enough to provide every person on board with three quarts a day, including that necessary "to boil provisions and to make gruel or other medicines prescribed by the ship's doctor." Nevertheless, on the first day out Bond gave orders that only a two-quart can of water was to be issued to each mess of six felons in the morning and another in the evening so that each man's allowance was no more than one pint of water every twenty-four hours. This ration was maintained for more than seven weeks regardless of the entreaties, not only of the felons themselves, but of William Warner, the ship's surgeon, and other officers who told Bond that such a small ration was insufficient to support life for so long. Even when convicts were obviously ill and received barley water or water gruel, Bond insisted that an equivalent amount of water should be withheld from their messes. The only additional liquid came in the form of boiled pease, wheat boiled in water with sugar twice a week, and oatmeal boiled in water "as thick as a spoon would stand upright in" twice a week.

The surgeon, however, found a way to give some of the sick a little extra water without Bond's knowledge. "When reduced to the utmost necessity, some found means to get salt water to drink and to cool their mouths." As the felons were allowed to come on deck they would beg Bond for water, showing him their dried and thickly furred tongues, "and some parched and cracked so deep they would contain a large quill." Even then, Bond beat them away, refusing to allow them any water though the ship had a fine voyage with fair winds. William Bird, a convict sentenced to transportation for suffocating his victims in the Round House at Westminster, wrote a note pleading for water to prevent his dying, but when Bond was shown it he exclaimed: "No, damn him, he murthered others in the same way, let him feel the smart himself."

Deponent John Wright, second mate of the *Justitia*, remembered that Bond would usually strike out at the felons who were continually crying and making a noise for water but, on two or three occasions during the voyage, he would give them a dram of gin. The ship's surgeon, corroborating the evidence of other witnesses, deposed that even when the heat was at its height, Bond would keep the felons cooped up below decks and feed them on salt provisions, saying he would not give them extra water until the ship neared land. The tongues of some of the victims appeared almost cleft and they frequently drank their own urine to relieve the pangs of thirst. During all this time, Warner insisted, the crew had all the water they wanted and the ship arrived in Maryland with nineteen large and four small casks of water unused.

Soon after leaving England, Bond discovered that some of the convicts still had money about them despite all the searches that had been made, and thereupon conferred upon Thomas Huddle, one of the felons aboard whom he trusted, the special privilege of walking the decks on condition that he took what money he could find from other felons when they fell to gambling in order to hand it over to Bond. As the ship neared Maryland, some demanded the return of the money confiscated from them. Not only did Bond refuse but he threatened to whip them for insubordination and to keelhaul any who would not give him half-a-crown. At this, a block was spliced to the yard arm and a rope attached to it, at the other end of which a spike was spliced. Beginning with a felon named Charles Tongue, each man was tied by the hands to the rope with his legs over the spike, drawn up to the yard arm and then dropped down into the sea two or three times. Even one of the women, Hannah White, who had just been delivered of a child, was threatened with this punishment but, overcome with terror, managed somehow to procure half-a-crown to secure her reprieve.

The deponents agreed that Bond had seen himself as "heir to all the felons that should die under his care" and, as soon as any of them were dead, he took everything they had and either kept or sold it. He had been seen to wear a pair of breeches that belonged to one of his dead passengers. The surgeon, in mitigation, added that occasionally Bond would give dead men's clothes to other felons who needed them. Chiefly because of the treatment they received on board, forty-five felons died on the *Justitia* between 23 April and 23 June 1743.

The only charges brought against John Sargent, captain of the *Forward*, were of robbery upon the high seas. Under examination, crew members related how felons aboard were brought up on deck during the voyage to Maryland, stripped down to their shirts, and searched for money or valuables. Finding a guinea on one felon, Sargent took possession of it, forcing him "to take gin in lieu thereof." When one of the women being transported was discovered to be carrying an order for the payment of two guineas in Maryland, she was invited by Sargent to take Geneva and gingerbread with him. He then relieved her of all her money by demanding two shillings a quart for the gin and a shilling a pound for cheese. Gin was sold on board to any convicts who could afford these inflated prices and, according to one deponent, more than forty died because of excessive drinking, "whereupon Captain Sargent sold their clothes at the mast for his private account."

Sargent's principal accuser was Catherine Davis, one of the few felons aboard his ship who appears to have had money and influence.[17] After she had been on the ship for several days in London, her husband, Lewis Davis, brought aboard two trunks for her use and presented Sargent with three guineas to ensure that Catherine would receive considerate treatment during the voyage. Since she was pregnant, Sargent agreed that "she might lie out her pregnancy in the steerage" rather than be confined with the other felons below. But, when her time came, she was herded in with the other women convicts on the pretext that Andrew Reid had ordered his captains not to entertain felons in the steerage for fear of their spreading infection among the ships' companies. Amidst the squalor of the convict hold Catherine was delivered of her child three weeks out from England: two weeks later the child was dead. Taking advantage of her condition, Sargent ordered Catherine Davis's possessions to be brought up on deck, ignoring her insistence that she had nothing that belonged to him. Sargent, however, took from her trunks four watches, some handkerchiefs, and three or four guineas, all of which he said he would take back to England as he believed them to have been stolen.

Catherine contrived to win the confidence and friendship of one of the *Forward*'s crew, Richard Gaudon, who testified that "when her child was delivered, the weather was very bad and the ship took on much water, and she was often thoroughly wetted in her bed, which gave her such colds and disorders that most of the ship's company imagined she would not live." Convinced herself that she would die, Catherine asked Gaudon to take charge of her goods but he, being afraid of Sargent, counselled her to put them in the care of the ship's doctor "as he was above being terrified by the Captain." As Catherine's condition worsened, Sargent said to Gaudon, "I am informed she has effects of value on board, do you know anything of them?" He swore he would prevent the doctor getting his hands on them. According to Gaudon, Catherine Davis had pleaded with Sargent that if he would only leave her some clothes, he could take whatever else he wanted.

Once arrived in Maryland, Sargent grew nervous for what he had done and put it about that Catherine Davis had made him a present of a number of things including two watches, even complaining: "It was a little enough present from a felon." And then he replaced some money in her trunk and asked Catherine for a written discharge which she at first refused on the grounds that she was unable to write, but was finally persuaded to make her mark.

All the charges against John Sargent were dismissed since the evidence against him was considered to lack weight, but Barnet Bond was arraigned at the Old Bailey on 27 April 1744 on four separate charges of murder on the high seas. His trial lasted from early morning until almost nine o'clock at night. Unfortunately no substantial record of the proceedings appears to have survived, the journals of the time believing the trial to be of such scant public interest that it was reported in very few lines. We learn merely, notwithstanding the impressive testimony against him, that Bond was honourably acquitted by the Old Bailey jury.[18] In the aftermath of these proceedings, John

Sargent brought a civil action against Andrew Reid for having
under-insured the *Forward*.[19] Catherine Davis, *alias* Mary Shirley,
was brought back to the Old Bailey to be tried on a charge of robbery,
was found guilty and, understandably, pleaded to be hanged rather
than be transported again.[20] Barnet Bond was never again employed
in the transportation trade, at least in England, for he settled in
Maryland where he died a few years later leaving his estates there
to his wife and children.[21]

The hardships incurred by women servants who braved, or who
were forced into, a long sea voyage in these times were common
enough to arouse no special attention save when a prosecution was
brought as the direct result. In 1750 a young girl by the name of
Elizabeth Hughes appeared before the High Court of Admiralty with
a complaint. In June 1749 she was hired by Joseph Scott in New
York to accompany him and his family on their passage to England
in his ship, the *Tryton*. She was quartered with the family in the
great cabin where she was required to sleep on the floor. Three days
out of New York, the captain of the ship, Archibald Ramidge, slipped
into her bedding "naked to his shirt . . . to lye with or have the
carnal knowledge of her body." When she cried out in alarm, Ramidge
swore the devil was in her and that he would have her put out of
the cabin. Elizabeth told her master the next morning of the incident
but he and his wife made a joke of it, saying: "She seems to think
much of being a bedfellow to the Captain, but before she comes to
England she won't think much of being a bedfellow to the whole
ship's crew." Scott added the observation that "it is the business of
every body on board to oblige the Captain." Mrs. Scott then gave
vent to complaints about the way Elizabeth washed the children's
clothes while her husband set about her with his cane, managing to
break her hand. Ramidge, looking on, called Elizabeth an ill-natured
creature, struck her on the mouth with enough force to break a tooth,
and dragged her on deck. "He wript open the foreparts of her gown
and shift, she having no stays on," and asked Scott whether she
should be whipped. Scott replied that he had dispensed with her
services and that Ramidge might do as he liked with her. On the
following Sunday morning the ship's carpenter fastened her down by
nailing her dress and stockings to the deck, put a rope under her
armpits and neck, and tied her head to an iron ring. So she lay all
day. That night Ramidge "thrust an iron spike into her privy parts
for not complying with his wishes . . . and then bade the crew to

view her." After he had intercourse with her where she lay, he allowed the mate and the boatswain to indulge themselves. Elizabeth was then confined for the remainder of the voyage between decks where, with the captain's permission, the rest of the crew had the use of her. One of them, John Esterby, who had taken advantage of Elizabeth for two or three days, confessed that others of the crew had shared her body. They had all found her drunk and troublesome so, to cool her off, they had tied her to the windlass and flung cold water over her.[22]

Sargent, Bond and Ramidge were far from being the only ships' masters whose crimes rivalled those of their passengers. John Lancey of Bideford, Devon, was employed by a merchant of that town as a captain of his ships and in 1752 was in charge of the *Nightingale* carrying fifteen convicts and a valuable cargo from Bideford to Maryland. Having fallen heavily into debt, Lancey hit on the idea of destroying the ship, blaming his seven-year passengers for the disaster, and collecting the insurance money. Accordingly, he made for the Isle of Lundy where he had a hole bored in the side of the ship, set it afire, and then ran round the decks loudly accusing the convicts of the mischief. The *Nightingale* sank, the captain and his crew and passengers were picked up by a passing Philadelphia ship, and all was going well until Lancey was betrayed by an accomplice. He was sentenced by the Court of Admiralty to hang in February 1754.[23]

A charge never levelled against the official transportation contractors, but one which was laid at the door of certain freebooting captains, was that of landing convicts in America in the guise of indentured servants. This practice, though of suspect legality, would clearly benefit all parties to the transaction except the unfortunate purchasers. In 1737 a Maryland newspaper reported "an arrant cheat at Annapolis when a vessel arrived there with a lading of convicts but equipped with sixty-six indentures signed by the Mayor of Dublin and twenty-two wigs of such a quality as to make it evident they were intended for no other use than to give the convicts a respectable appearance and the best chance of being sold as free servants."[24] In 1749 Peter Montgomery made a deposition declaring that he was present in Belfast in September 1748 when two convicts, Katherine and Mary McKoy, were delivered by James Potts, merchant, to the *Eagle*, under Mr. Oliver Airy, to be shipped to Boston. For a while they were confined under decks as befitted their status but, since they were known to be good spinners, the captain bribed his crew to conceal their background in order that they might be sold as servants.[25] Such dissembling appears to have been connived at even by Crown officials, for the shipping returns made from Virginia in the period 1760-70 record the cargoes of known convict ships simply as "European goods"![26]

The last word on the condition of convict ships must be given to Governor Horatio Sharpe of Maryland who protested at the great number of people who were being wiped out by the jail fever brought over by "servants" from on board crowded, infectious ships. He wrote to London on 27 July 1767:

> Contractors who have only a certain number of vessels in the Maryland Trade must it seems at particular times empty the jails and by that means it sometimes happens that they oblige the masters of their ships to receive on board twice the number they ought to bring, little anxious themselves of the consequences to the inhabitants here, nor very solicitous whether or no the crowding too great a number of the poor wretches into small compass may not be the means of destroying some of them.[27]

He went on to quote from a report made to him by his agent George Selwyn after he had inspected one of John Stewart's ships which was about to sail for Maryland:

> I went on board and, to be sure, all the horror I ever had an idea of is short of what I saw this poor man in; chained to a board in a hole not above 16 feet long, more than 50 with him, a collar and padlock about his neck, and chained to five of the most dreadful creatures I ever looked on.[28]

NOTES

1. *National Genealogical Society Quarterly*, Vol. 63 (1975), pp. 172-175.

2. See, for example, Sir Walter Besant, *Survey of London — London in the Eighteenth Century* (London, 1902), p. 557.

3. The *Maryland Gazette* of 23 August 1764, for example, cites a certain ship's captain who preserved discipline on his ship by "firing among the convicts and bleeding a few."

4. The transportation contractors were chary of accepting convicts who failed to conform to standard specifications. In 1743 a contractor wrote to the Derbyshire justices about one such prisoner: "If he be large and old I cannot take him under £5." See John C. Cox, *Three Centuries of Derbyshire Annals* (London, 1890), Vol. I, p. 57.

5. Marcellus Rivers and Oxenbridge Foyle, *England's Slavery or Barbados Merchandize* (London, 1659); see also Thomas Burton, *Diary*, ed. John T. Rutt (London, 1828), Vol. IV, pp. 255-259. Their case was debated in the English Parliament.

6. John Coad, *Memorandum of the Wonderful Providence of God* (London, 1849), pp. 23-27.

7. *Acts of Privy Council (Colonial) 1720-1745*, p. 630.

8. Daniel Defoe, *op. cit.*, pp. 301-307.

9. A version printed in London in about 1800 renders the author's name correctly as James Revel; another version issued in Dublin some twenty years later wrongly transliterates the name as Ruel. Copy by courtesy of the Irish State Paper Office.

10. British Library Add. Mss. 27,826: Place Tracts.

11. PRO (Public Record Office): Chancery Proceedings, C11/1223/28. Letter from George Tilly, Virginia, to Jonathan Forward, London, 2 August 1725.

12. Few of the ships used in the transportation trade seem to have been specially built for the purpose though many were adapted. The last *Justitia* to ply the trade was registered in London in 1764 as a French prize, probably a slave ship, of 305 tons and a crew of sixteen; see PRO: Treasury Papers, T1/461.

13. PRO: Chancery Proceedings, C11/1886/36.

14. *Ibid.*, C11/2499/19.

15. PRO: Admiralty Papers, ADM 2/1054/195-213.

16. PRO: High Court of Admiralty Papers, HCA 1/57/36 and 85-96.

17. *Ibid.*, HCA 1/19/124 ff.

18. *C.f. The London Magazine* which reported the case in one sentence.

19. PRO: Chancery Proceedings, C11/557/28.

20. Old Bailey Sessions Papers for May 1744.

21. PRO: Will of Barnet Bond, PCC 100/1749.

22. PRO: High Court of Admiralty Papers, HCA 1/57/128 and 58/1.

23. *Tyburn Chronicle* (London, 1768), Vol. 1.

24. Edward D. Neill, *Terrae Mariae* (Philadelphia, 1867), p. 203.

25. *American Historical Review*, Vol. 2 (1896), p. 22.

26. PRO: Colonial Office Papers, CO 5/1449-1450.

27. Basil Sollers, *op. cit.*, p. 40.

27. *Ibid.*, p. 41.

CHAPTER IX

The New Immigrants

Felons exiled into the colonies were frequently spoken of, both by themselves and by their jailers, as having been sent or sold into slavery.[1] That this was not just a figure of hyperbole becomes evident upon reading contemporary accounts based on personal experience. Rivers and Foyle, the political exiles whose account of their voyage to Barbados has already been quoted, describe their reception in the island in 1656:

> The Master of the ship sold your miserable Petitioners and the others, the generality of them to the most inhumane and barbarous persons for 1550 pound weight of sugar apiece (more or less according to their working faculties) . . . neither sparing the aged of threescore and sixteen years old, nor Divines, nor Officers, nor Gentlemen, nor any age or condition of men, but rendered all alike in this most insupportable Captivity, they now generally grinding at the Mills, attending furnaces, or digging in this scorching island, having nothing to feed on — notwithstanding their hard labour — but potato roots, nor to drink but water with such roots mashed in it . . . being bought and sold still from one planter to another, or attached as horses and beasts for the debts of their masters, being whipped at the whipping posts as rogues for their masters' pleasure, and sleep in styes worse than hogs in England, and many other ways made miserable beyond expression or Christian imagination.[2]

Richard Ligon, perhaps a more detached observer, embarked in London on 16 June 1647 on the *Achilles*, under Mr. Thomas Crowder, for Barbados and found the ship to be carrying "many servant women, the major part of them from Bridewell . . . and such like places of education." He observed after his arrival:

The island [of Barbados] is divided into three sorts of men, *viz.* masters, servants and slaves. The slaves and their posterity, being subject to their masters for ever, are kept and preserved with greater care than the servants who are there but for five years ... For the time the servants have the worse lives, for they are but to very hard labour, ill lodging, and their diet very slight ... Truly I have seen such cruelty done to servants as I could not think one Christian could have done to another: but as discreeter and better-natured have come to rule there, the servants' lives have been much bettered, for now most of the servants lie in hammocks and in warm rooms; and, when they come in wet, have shifts of shirts and drawers, which is all the clothes they wear, and are fed with bone meat twice or thrice a week.[3]

The demand for new labour in the island was such that, according to a visitor there in 1655:

The custom of all merchants trading thither is to bring as many men and women as they can. No sooner doth a ship come to an anchor but presently the islanders go aboard her inquiring what servants they can buy. If they are above seventeen years of age, they serve but four years [but] if under seventeen, then left to the discretion of the merchant as he can agree with the planter. These servants planteth, weedeth, and manureth their ground, all by hand.[4]

Contemporary accounts of a servant's or transported felon's life in mainland America are little different. Though many, undoubtedly, had the good fortune to be sold to kind and considerate masters, their stories have largely gone untold. One of the earliest letters on record from a servant in Virginia is that from Richard Frethorne (*Frethram* in the 1624 Virginia Census) of Martin's Hundred written to his parents in London on 2 and 3 April 1623 to tell them that since he had landed,

I have eaten nothing but pease and loblolly [water-gruel] and have had to work both early and late for a mess of water gruel and a mouthful of bread and beef; a mouthful of bread for a penny loaf cannot serve four men. I had eaten more in a day at home than was allowed for a week in Virginia, and you had often given more than my present allowance to a beggar at your door. I have nothing at all, not even a shirt, only one poor suit, a pair of shoes and stockings. The people cried out "Oh that they were in England without their limbs" as they begged from door to door. There is nothing to be got but sickness and death, except that we had money to lay out in some things for profit. Oh that you did see my daily and hourly sighs and groans, tears and thumps that I afford mine own breast, and rue and curse the hour of my birth with holy Job. I had thought no head had been able to hold so much water as hath and doth daily flow from my eyes.

When one of the settlers heard Frethorne was a servant of the Virginia Company, he remarked: "You had been better knocked on the head." Frethorne died shortly after writing this letter.[5]

The new arrivals in Virginia were described to Moll Flanders by her mother:

The greatest part of the inhabitants came thither in very indifferent circumstances from England . . . Generally speaking, they were of two sorts; either, first, such as were brought over by the masters of ships to be sold as servants . . . but they are more properly called slaves; or secondly, such as are transported from Newgate and other prisons . . . When they come here, we make no difference; the planters buy them, and they work together in the fields till their time is out. When 'tis expired they have encouragement given them to plant for themselves, for they have a certain number of acres of land allotted them by the country . . . and the tradesmen and merchants will trust them with tools and clothes and other necessaries upon the credit of their crop before it is grown . . . Hence, many a Newgate-bird becomes a great man, and we have several justices of the peace, officers of the trained bands, and magistrates of the towns they live in, that have been burnt in the hand . . . There are more thieves and rogues made by that one prison of Newgate than by all the clubs and societies of villains in the nation; 'tis that cursed place . . . that half peoples this colony.[6]

Once the felons were landed in America:

In short time men up to us came,
Some ask'd our trades and others ask'd our names.
Some view'd our limbs and others turn'd us round,
Examining (like horses) if we were sound,
What trade are you my lad?, says one to me,
A Tin-man, Sir, that will not do said he.

Some felt our hands and view'd our legs and feet,
and made us walk to see if we were compleat.
Some view'd our teeth to see if they were good,
or fit to chew our hard and homely food.

If any lik'd our looks or limbs or trade,
The Captain then a good advantage made,
For they a difference made it did appear,
'Twixt those for seven and those for fourteen years.

Another difference too there is allow'd.
They who have money have most favour shew'd,
For if no cloaths nor money have they got,
Hard is their fate and hard will be their lot.

At length a grim old man unto me came,
He ask'd my trade and likewise my name,
I told him I a Tin-man was by trade,
And not quite eighteen years of age I said.

Likewise the cause I told that brought me there,
That I for fourteen years transported were,
And when he this from me did understand,
He bought me of the captain out of hand.

Down to the harbour I was took again,
On board a sloop, and loaded with a chain,
Which I was forc'd to wear both night and day,
For fear I from the sloop should get away.

My Master was a man but of ill fame,
Who first of all a transport thither came.
In Rappahannock county he did dwell
Up Rappahannock river it's known well.

And when the sloop with loading home was sent,
An hundred miles he up the river went
The weather cold and very hard my fare,
My lodging on the deck both hard and bare.

At last to my new master's house I came,
At the town of Wicomoco call'd by name,
Where my Europian cloaths were took from me,
Which never after I again did see.

A canvas shirt and trousers then they gave,
And a hopsack frock in which I was to slave,
No shoes, no stockings had I for to wear,
Nor hat nor cap both head and feet were bare.

Thus drest into the field I next must go,
Amongst Tobacco plants all day to hoe,
At day break in the morning our work begun,
And so held to the setting of the sun.

My fellow slaves were just five transports more,
With nineteen Negros which were twenty four,
Besides four transport women in the house,
To wait upon his daughter and his spouse.

We and the negroes all alike did fear,
Of work and food we had an equal share,
For in a piece of ground we call'd our own,
The food we eat first by ourselves were sown.

No other time to us they did allow,
But on a Sunday we the same must do,
Six days we slave for our master's good.
The seventh day is to produce our food.

Sometimes when we a hard day's work have done,
Away unto the mill we must be gone
Till twelve or one O'Clock a grinding corn,
Yet must be up at day light in the morn.

And if we offer for to run away,
For every hour we must serve a day,
For every day a week, they're so severe,
For every week a month, for every month a year.

For in publick places they'll put up your name,
That every one their just demands may claim.
But if they murder rob or steal when there,
They're straightway hang'd the laws are so severe,
For by the rigour of that very law,
They're much kept under and do stand in awe.

At length it pleased God I sick did fal
But I no favour could receive at all,
For I was forc'd to work while I could stand,
Or hold the hoe within my feeble hand.

Much hardship then indeed I did endure,
No dog was ever used so I'm sure.
More pity the poor Negro slaves bestow'd,
Than my inhuman brutal Master shew'd.

*　　*　　*

And but two more [years] by law I had to stay,
When death did for our cruel master call,
But that was no relief to us at all.
The widow could not the Plantation hold,
So we and that was both for to be sold.

A lawyer rich who at James-Town did dwell,
Came down to view and lik'd it very well.
He bought the Negroes who for life were slaves,
But no transported felons would he have,
So we were put like sheep into a fold,
There unto the best bidder to be sold.[7]

The remaining verses by James Revel describe how he was purchased by a gentleman and served out the remainder of his time in
relative ease before returning to his family in England. He ended his
lay with a warning:

Altho' but little crimes you here have done,
Consider seven or fourteen years to come,
Forc'd from your friends and country for to go,
Amongst the Negro's to work at the hoe,
In distant countries void of all relief,
Sold for a slave because you prov'd a thief.

Therefore young men with speed your lives amend,
Take my advice as one that is your friend,
For tho' so slight you make of it here,
Hard is your lot if once they get you there.

Revel's account is accurate enough in those details which can be
verified to support the assumption that it is based on true experience.

The Old Bailey Sessions Papers, for the enlightenment of its readers,
described the manner in which convicts were sold in America:

They are placed together in a Row, like so many oxen or cows,
and the Planters come and survey them; and if they like 'em,
they agree for price with the person entrusted with the selling of
'em. And after they have paid the money, they ask 'em if they
like him for a Master and is willing to go with him. If they
answer in the Affirmative, they are delivered to him as his
Property. If on the contrary, as sometimes happens, they should
answer in the Negative, the Planter has his Money again and
another Planter may make choice of him, whom he may likewise
refuse, but no more, for with the Third it seems, he is obliged

to go, whether he likes him or not. As there are frequently People
who run away from their Masters, there is a reward of twenty
shillings paid for the taking of 'em, which makes it very difficult
for 'em to escape. When a Master gives them a discharge, he
always gives them a Pass, by the Authority of which they may
safely go anywhere: and, without one, they are liable to be put
into a Gaol and confin'd for some days to see if any Enquiry be
made after them.[8]

Some twenty years later the scene had changed little. William
Green, convicted at Nottingham in 1762 and transported from London
to Maryland by the *Sally*, described his arrival:

We were put ashore in couples chained together and driven in
lots like oxen or sheep [to be inspected by purchasers who] search
us there as the dealers in horses do these animals in the country,
by looking at our teeth, viewing our limbs to see if they are
sound and fit for their labour, and if they approve of us after
asking our trades and names and what crimes we have been guilty
of to bring us to that shame, the bargain is made.[9]

A contemporary letter from an indentured servant, William Eddis,
described how "these unhappy beings [transported convicts] are
consigned to an agent who classes them suitably to their real or
supposed qualifications, advertises them for sale, and disposes of
them for seven years to planters, mechanics and such as choose to
retain them for domestic service." He commented on how few of
those who survived their period of enforced labour settled in their
own neighbourhood: "The stamp of infamy was too strong upon them
and they therefore either returned to Europe to renew their life of
crime or, if they had imbibed habits of honesty and industry, removed
to a distant situation in the hope that they might remain unknown."[10]

The American newspapers of the time regularly advertised
forthcoming auctions of newly imported felons along the lines of the
following from the *Maryland Gazette* of 24 November 1768:

Just imported from Bristol in the ship *Randolph*, Captain John
Weber Price, one hundred and fifteen convicts, men, women, and
lads: Among whom are several tradesmen, who are to be sold
on board the said ship, now in Annapolis Dock, this day and
Saturday next by Smith & Sadler.

Perhaps the cream of the felons arriving in America was represented by those managing to pass themselves off as well-educated, as many had set themselves up to be in order to become competent swindlers. However, the demand in the southern colonies for literate servants appears to have been rather less than for manual workers. Rev. Jonathan Boucher went so far as to complain:

> Two thirds of the little education we receive [in Maryland] are derived from instructors who are either indented servants or transported felons. Not a ship arrives, either with redemptioners or convicts, in which schoolmasters are not as regularly advertised for sale as weavers, tailors, or any other trade; with little other difference that I can hear of, excepting perhaps that the former do not normally fetch so good a price as the latter.[11]

In the latter years of British colonial rule, so-called soul drivers would board the convict ships to purchase groups of felons whom they would then drive through the countryside like a flock of sheep, selling them along the wayside whenever opportunity offered.

The best description of a felon's new life in America probably comes from the pen of Bampfylde Moore Carew, a man of gentle birth and some culture, who, having turned rogue, told his story with the wit and good humour befitting his station. When sentenced at the Devon Quarter Sessions in 1738 to be transported to "Merry-land," he informed the justice that "he apprehended it ought to be pronounced 'Maryland,'" and added for good measure that "as he was desirous of seeing that country, the sentence would save him five pounds for his passage." Of thirty-five offenders brought to trial with him, thirty-two were given a similar sentence, which provoked him to comment: "Whether, at this period of time, Mankind were more profligate than usual, or whether there was a more than ordinary demand for Men in his Majesty's Colonies, cannot by us be determined."

The transport ship carrying Carew and his fellow convicts having reached Talbot County:

> The Captain ordered a Gun to be fired as a Signal for the Planters to come down, and then went ashore; he soon after sent on board a Hogshead of Rum and order'd all the Men Convicts to be close shaved against the next Morning, and the Women to have their best Head Dresses put on, which occasion'd no little Hurry on board, for between the Trimming of Beards and the putting on of Caps, all hands were fully employed. In the morning the

> Captain ordered publick Notice to be given of a Day of Sale;
> the Convicts, who were pretty near a Hundred, were all ordered
> upon Deck, where a large Bowl of Punch was made, and the
> Planters flock'd on board.

Once they had collected any letters addressed to them, the planters
set about examining and selecting suitable servants amongst the
convicts and pressed the captain for details of any joiners, carpenters,
blacksmiths, weavers and tailors there might be amongst them.

Carew contrived to make his escape from the ship before the auction
was completed but was recaptured and hauled before the captain who

> received him with a great deal of malicious Satisfaction in his
> Countenance . . . and, with a tyrannic tone, bid him Strip, calling
> to his Boatswain to bring up the Cat o' Nine Tails and tie him
> up to the main Gears: accordingly our Hero was obliged to
> undergo a cruel and shameful punishment.

He was then taken ashore to visit a blacksmith who was ordered
to fit him with a heavy iron collar "which in Maryland they call a
Pot-Hook, and is usually put about the Necks of the runaway Slaves."
When it was welded round his neck, the captain jeered, "Now run
away if you can!" Ever resourceful, Carew won the sympathy and
assistance of some captains of the other ships then in port and was
able to steal away at night into the mountains. There he struck up
a friendship with some Indians who removed his collar, enabling
him, like many a convict before and after him, to make his way into
Pennsylvania. From there, and after a tour of New York, he shipped
home again to England.[12]

Then, as now, the boundary between fact and fiction could be
blurred to satisfy the tastes of those who chose to read lurid tales
of life in the far West. When such a tale is told by a "young
nobleman" sold into slavery by a wicked uncle, further caution may
be necessary. The author, James Annesley, who claimed to be a
nephew of the Earl of Anglesey, worked on a plantation in Newcastle
County (Delaware) with other slaves cutting timber to make pipe
staves.

> Nothing is indeed more strange than that any who have known
> a better State can support with Life the Hardships of an American
> Slavery which is infinitely more terrible than that of a Turkish

one . . . for, besides the incessant toil they undergo, the Nature of their Labour is such that they are obliged to be continually exposed to the Air, which is unwholesome enough, the Heats and Colds which the different Seasons of the year bring on in these Parts being far greater than any we know in Europe. Then, after being allowed no Shelter from either of these Extremes, all the Refreshment afforded them is *Poue*, or a sort of Bread made with Indian Corn, heavy on the Stomach and insipid to the Palate, with a Draught of Water, or at best mingled with a little Ginger or Molasses, both of which are made of the same kind of Corn, is set before them, moistened with the Fat of Bacon or Hog's Lard . . . Some Masters there are that appear more human . . . and soften in some measure the Severity of those poor Creatures' Fate by gentle Words.

He then tells the story of a female slave of nearly sixty, formerly the wife of a man of substance in England who disposed of her by having her kidnapped and shipped off to Pennsylvania. This woman was required to feed the field workers on the plantation which meant a walk of many miles each day and, because of her weak constitution, she would faint many times on her rounds. When she wrote home to England for money with which to purchase her freedom, she was beaten. Escape from an indefinite slavery was therefore impossible for

it is a sort of barbarous policy in these Planters to use their Slaves ill, especially when the Time for which they are bound is near expired, because by the Laws of that Country, when any of them run away, if they are retaken, as they commonly are, they are mulcted for that Disobedience and oblig'd to pay by a longer Servitude all the Expenses and Damages the Master pretends he has sustained by their Elopement, so that by this means some of them serve double the years they were contracted for.

As a punishment for stealing money, one indentured servant was tied to a post and whipped, thrown into a dungeon for four days, and then sold to another planter. When the hero of the story attempted to escape himself, he was captured, taken to court, and exposed in the market place of Chestertown every day for five weeks to be reclaimed. When eventually his old master caught up with him, he was treated even more harshly than before.[13]

Though the details of the story may be open to question, there can be no doubt that transported convicts and indentured servants were always at risk of a fate similar to that of the young nobleman. When Sir John Fielding wrote to the Earl of Suffolk in 1773 he acknowledged that the penalty of transportation was one which created terror, basing his opinion on first-hand accounts of those who had suffered in the American colonies.[14]

Attempted escape from servitude was punished ferociously. In Virginia thirty-nine lashes of the whip were prescribed for the offence;[15] in Maryland ten days' additional service could be exacted for every day of freedom;[16] while in South Carolina, at one time, the penalty was twenty-eight days' service for every day of absence.[17] By 1744 the punishment in South Carolina had been softened to one week's service for every day of absence, but a fugitive could receive the additional penalty of twenty lashes of the whip. These, of course, were penalties prescribed by law, but no regulation limited the beatings and deprivations which might be imposed on servants at a master's mere whim. Pennsylvania was the nearest haven in which a servant escaping from the South might find safe refuge.

The difficulty of making a successful escape should not, however, be underestimated. Without formal discharge papers, any wanderer could be apprehended and questioned, and rewards were offered for the capture of absconding servants. American newspapers carried frequent advertisements such as the following, printed in 1722:

> Ran away from Rev. D. Magill, Upper Marlborough, Maryland, a servant, clothed with damask breeches and vest, black broadcloth coat, broadcloth cloak of copper colour, lined and trimmed with black, and wearing black stockings.[18]

Few runaways would have been so elegantly attired; many, including women, would have been instantly recognised by their fetters. One of these, Hannah Boyer, aged twenty-three, ran away from her master in 1752 still wearing a horse-lock and chain on one leg. On 9 April in the same year the *Maryland Gazette* ran the following notice:

> Cecil County, Maryland. Ran away last Night, from the Subscriber, a Convict Servant Man, named *Jacob Parrott* [sentenced in Cornwall in March 1749], a West Country Man, aged about 23 Years, of a fair Complexion, short but well set, and very

saucy: He took with him a new Felt Hat, (and perhaps an old
Leather Cap) a good Duffel Coat, with large white Metal Buttons,
a good ash coloured Kersey Coat, with a black Cape, and carv'd
white Metal Buttens, a brown Holland Jacket without Sleeves,
double breasted, with yellow wash'd Buttons, a Pair of half worn
Buff Breeches,a Pair of white Cotton Stockings, a Pair of grey
Yarn Hose lately footed,a Pair of new Pumps, a Pair of old Shoes,
a Pair of large Pewter Buckles, with Brass Anchors and Tongues,
a Dowglass and white Linnen Shirt. He is supposed to make for
Annapolis or intends to cross the Bay for *Baltimore* County. All
Masters of Vessels are warned at their Peril, not to carry him
off. He has been a Footman in *England*; and being a dextrous
Fellow, may pretend to be a Coachman, Gardener, Sawyer, Shoemaker, &c. He took with him a Brown Horse, Bridle and Saddle;
but probably will exchange the Horse for some other. Whoever
secures the said Servant, so that he and the Cloaths may be had
again, shall have Twenty Shillings more than the Law allows,
paid by . . . *Hugh Jones.*

Advertisements in the Maryland newspapers for runaway convict
servants would often disclose not only their names and aliases but
state place of birth, age, physical characteristics and occupation, the
Gazette observing that only those convicts who were "wicked and
bad" generally attempted to escape, "whilst those more innocent, and
who come for very light offenses, serve their time out here, behave
well, and become useful People."[19]

Escaped convicts could also bring financial loss to the ships'
captains who brought them to America. Thomas Boyd, Master of the
Prince Royale, wrote from Cork on 7 June 1723 to the Town Clerk
of Sandwich, Kent:

Enclosed you have a certificate for landing of Solomon Huffam,
transported in my ship . . . in the year 1721 to Virginia. I hope
that on receipt hereof, you'd be so kind as to cancel my bond
given you for his effectual transportation. About 3 moneths after
sale he ran away from his master, one Thomas Pulleyne in
Rappahannock River, and has not been since heard of.[20]

If a transported felon made his appearance back in England before
his term expired he was constrained to remain in hiding or go on
the run for, if he was apprehended, his offence carried an automatic
death penalty. The rewards paid for successful prosecution of felons

made England a very unsafe place for anyone returning too early from transportation. Therefore, while the number who contrived to get home was small in relation to the total number transported, they tended to belong mainly to the professional class of criminals whose activities in England gave rise to the imposition of special measures against them. One John Poulter, *alias* Baxter, was persuaded in 1753 to turn King's evidence and achieved notoriety in securing the apprehension of "a numerous gang of villains."

While awaiting the death sentence in Ivelchester Jail for having robbed a man in Salisbury, Poulter wrote an account of his life as a member of a gang of thieves during the previous five years when he had exercised no profession other than that of a criminal. He wrote down details of all his associates, fences and receivers and gave the names of all the thirty-one men he knew to have returned from transportation before the end of their terms. His confessions were published[21] and his book caused a sensation, going into seven editions within a year and reaching a twelfth edition by 1761. If Poulter had hoped by his full confession to escape the full severity of the law, he was sadly disappointed, and when he learned of his sentence he attempted to escape but was soon caught and hanged.

As part of his confession Poulter submitted for public consideration his own suggestions for preventing the return of convicts from transportation, and described the ways in which they most commonly made their escape from slavery:

> The general way is this: just before they go on board a ship, their friend or Accomplices purchase them their freedom from the Merchant or Captain that belongs to the said ship for above Ten Pounds Sterling, some gives more and some less. Then the friends of the convict or convicts gets a note from the Merchant or Captain that the person is free to go unmolested when the ships arrive between the Capes of Virginia, where they please. But I never heard of any convict that came home again in the same ship they went over in; for the Merchant or Captain gives a bond to the Sheriff of the Country where such Convicts go from, to leave them in America, and they get a Receipt from the Custom there, but as there are ships coming home every week, if they can pay their passage back again, and them that cannot free themselves take an opportunity of running away from their Master, and lay in the woods by day and travel by night for Philadelphia, New York, or Boston, in which places no questions are asked of them. This encourages a great many to commit

robberies more than they would because they say they do not mind Transportation, it being but four or five months' pleasure, for they can get their Freedom and come home again. I know one that went over but bribed some of the Ship's Crew lying in the Transport Hole, Bristol. Her name was Elizabeth Connor. I think it was in 1748 she was convicted at the said City for picking pockets and was ordered for Transportation, but is now in England.

For those blessed with money, transportation could, at most, be an inconvenience. They would ride in cheerful consort with the contractor in his carriage to the ship, take up their quarters in a private cabin, spend the voyage in sociable indolence, and spend only as much time at the port of landing as it took to arrange their freedom and passage onwards. Jenny Diver, *alias* Young (see chapter X for some further account of her), before she was hanged at Tyburn in 1741, was

a notorious thief who, fifteen years before, operated with a desperate gang of robbers. Being at last apprehended in 1738 and sentenced to be transported, she spent her four months' waiting time in Newgate as a fence and bought such things as came her way, having money and knowing the business could in no way affect her, she being cast already; and when she went away she had as many goods of one sort or another as would almost have loaded a wagon and took them aboard the ship. The goods were neither examined nor detained. When she came aboard, she was treated in quite a different way from the rest of the transports and was put ashore at the first port they came to in Virginia, that is she was landed as a passenger who came to Virginia voluntarily. She stayed no longer than to see the country, for business in her way could not be transacted there. So, after she had devoted herself as long as she thought proper, she agreed with a gentleman for her passage to England. It does not appear she was ever molested on account of her having returned from transportation.[22]

Another contemporary observer complained:

Our subtle criminals have found out means to render transportation ineffectual. Some have escaped on the voyage itself, others have never been put on board, several have reached the plantations but returned by the first ship. Those that are forced to stay do very little service themselves and spoil the other slaves, teaching the African more villainy and mischief than ever they could have learned without their example and instruction. . . The mild usage our felons receive beyond sea . . . has quite destroyed the end which transportation was designed for. The criminals have no dread against it.[23]

Amongst the more fortunate emigrants in bondage must surely be counted William Duell. He was sentenced in 1739 to be hanged and, in accordance with the custom then prevailing, his body was afterwards handed over to the surgeons to be dissected in the interests of medical science. When he had been taken down from the gibbet and carted to Surgeons' Hall, he came back to life on the dissecting table to the astonishment of all present. He was doubly blessed since the capital sentence was then commuted to transportation for life and he departed for America early in 1740.

Equally grotesque in its own way, but a story which deserves repetition, is that of Sarah Wilson who

waited upon Miss Vernon, sister to Lady Grosvenor and maid of honour to the queen. She, having found means to be admitted to one of the royal apartments, took occasion to break open a cabinet and rifled it of many valuable jewels, for which she was apprehended, tried, and condemned to die; but through the interposition of her mistress, her sentence was softened into transportation. Accordingly, in the fall of 1771, she was landed in Maryland where she was exposed to sale and purchased. After a short residence in that place, she very secretly decamped and escaped into Virginia, travelled through that colony and through North to South Carolina. When at a proper distance from her purchaser, she assumed the title of The Princess Susanna Carolina Matilda, pronouncing herself to be an own sister to our sovereign lady the queen. She had carried with her clothes that served to favour the deception and had secured a part of the jewels together with Her Majesty's picture. She travelled from one gentleman's house to another under these pretences, making astonishing impressions in many places, affecting the mode of royalty so inimitably that many had the honour to kiss her hand. To some she promised governments, to others regiments, with promotions of all kinds in the treasury, army, and the royal navy. In short, she acted her part so plausibly as to persuade the generality that she was no impostor. In vain did many sensible gentlemen in those parts exert themselves to detect and make a proper example of her; for she had levied heavy contributions upon some persons of the highest rank in the southern colonies. At length, however,

an advertisement appeared, and a messenger arrived from her
master who raised a loud hue and cry for her serene highness.
The lady was then on an excursion of a few miles to a neighbouring plantation, for which place the messenger had set out
when the gentleman who brought this information left Charles
Town.[24]

Sarah Wilson had, perhaps, heard of or read the *Life of the Famous
Madam Charlton* who had charmed the whole of London a century
before. This lady arrived in the capital from Holland in 1661, claiming
to have been born at Cologne, Germany, the daughter of Henry van
Wolway, Lord of Holmstein, and to be heiress to a large fortune.
Other accounts described her as the daughter of the Duke of Oudenia
but, to polite London society she was known familiarly as "The
German Princess." With these credentials she was able to dupe many
willing victims. Her fame spread further when she was prosecuted
on a charge of bigamy, of which she was acquitted, and went on to
take the leading part in a specially-composed play called, inevitably,
The German Princess. After he had seen this production in 1664,
Samuel Pepys said of it: "Never was any thing done in earnest worse
performed in jest." Mary Moders (for that was her real name) next
turned common thief, was apprehended, sentenced, and in February
1671 transported to Jamaica from where, after a short residence, she
returned to England, there to be hanged in 1673. By her own
confession she was, in fact, the daughter of a cathedral chorister in
Canterbury, Kent.

Few transported felons or indentured servants in America can have
had such exotic tales to relate to their families and friends, and the
condition of many of them who have passed from history without a
mark is, perhaps, best described in a poignant letter from Elizabeth
Spriggs in Maryland to her father, Mr. John Spriggs, whitesmith of
White Cross Street, Cripplegate, London, dated 22 September 1756:

Honoured Father,

My being for ever banished from your sight will, I hope, pardon
the boldness I now take of troubling you with these. My long
silence has been purely owing to my undutifulness to you, and
well knowing I had offended in the highest degree put a tie to
my tongue and pen for fear I should be extinct from your good
graces and add a further trouble to you. But too well knowing
your care and tenderness for me so long as I retained my duty

to you, induced me once again to endeavour, if possible, to kindle up that flame again. O Dear Father, believe what I am going to relate, the words of truth and sincerity, and balance my former bad conduct [against] my sufferings here, and then I am sure you'll pity your distressed daughter.

What we unfortunate English people suffer here is beyond the probability of you in England to conceive. Let it suffice that I, one of the unhappy number, am toiling almost day and night, and very often in the horses' drudgery, with only this comfort that: "You bitch, you do not half enough:" and then tied up and whipped to that degree that you'd not serve an animal; scarce anything but Indian corn and salt to eat, and that even begrudged. Nay, many negroes are better used: almost naked, no shoes or stockings to wear, and the comfort after slaving during Master's pleasure what rest we can get is to wrap ourselves in a blanket and lie upon the ground.

This is the deplorable condition your poor Betty endures, and now I beg, if you have any bowels of compassion left, show it by sending me some relief. Clothing is the principal thing wanting, which if you should condescend to, may easily send them to me by any of the ships bound to Baltimore Town, Patapsco River, Maryland. And give me leave to conclude my duty to you and uncles and aunts, and respect to all friends, Honoured Father.

Your undutiful and disobedient child,
Elizabeth Sprigs.

Please direct for me at Mr. Richard Cross to be left at Mr. Lux's, merchant in Baltimore Town.[25]

Fate had a last bitter blow for Elizabeth Spriggs: her letter never reached her father for the ship carrying it was seized by the French and they, in turn, were taken prize by an English warship which deposited all the captured correspondence, French and English, with the Admiralty.

NOTES

1. Modern writers on criminology have not hesitated, as the result of their own researches, to reach the same conclusion: *c.f.* Ann D. Smith who, in her book *Women in Prison* (London, 1962), p. 67, writes: "Transportation became, in fact, a branch of the slave trade . . . and it was only when the African slave trade brought even cheaper labour to the colonies that the trade in convicts languished."

2. *Op.cit.*, British Library E1833.

3. Richard Ligon, *History of Barbados* (London, 1673), pp. 43-44.

4. Historical Manuscripts Commission: *Seventh Report*, Appendix 5: Letter from F. Barrington to Sir John Barrington.

5. Royal Commission on Historical Manuscripts: *Eighth Report*, Appendix Part II, p.409.

6. Daniel Defoe, *Moll Flanders*, *op. cit.*, pp. 89-90.

7. James Revel, *op. cit.*

8. Old Bailey Sessions Papers for November 1744, footnote.

9. William Green, chapbook titled *The Sufferings of W.G. . .* (London, 1774).

10. William Eddis, *Letters from America* (Cambridge, Mass., 1969), pp. 66-67.

11. Jonathan Boucher, *The American Revolution in Thirteen Discourses* (London, 1797), pp. 183-184.

12. *The Life and Adventures of Bamfylde Moore Carew . . . as Related by Himself During His Passage to the Plantations in America* (Exeter, 1745). Carew was the son of Rev. Theodore Carew of Bickley, near Tiverton, Devon, born in 1693 and named after his godfather, Hon. Hugh Bampfylde, and after Hon. Major Moore.

13. *Memoirs of a Young Nobleman Return'd from a Thirteen Years Slavery in America, Where He Had Been Sent by the Wicked Contrivances of His Cruel Uncle* (London, 1743).

14. *Calendar of State Papers Domestic 1773-1775* (London, 1899).

15. William W. Hening, *Statutes of Virginia*, Vol. 2 (1823).

16. Thomas Bacon, *Laws of Maryland* (Annapolis, 1765).

17. Edward Channing, *op. cit.*, Vol. 2.

18. Edward D. Neill, *op. cit.*, p. 213.

19. I am indebted for the details that appeared in Maryland newspapers to Richard J. Cox, "Maryland Runaway Convict Servants 1745-1780," *National Genealogical Society Quarterly*, Vol. 68 (1980), pp. 105-114, 232-233, and Vol. 69 (1981), pp. 51-58, 125-132, 205-214, 293-300.

20. Kent Records, Q/SOW1 f.98.

21. *Newgate Trials*, Vol. 6: The Discovery of John Poulter, *alias* Baxter.

22. Place Papers, *op.cit.*

23. Bernard de Mandeville, *op. cit*, pp. 46-48.

24. *London Magazine*, Vol. 42 (1773).

25. PRO (Public Record Office): High Court of Admiralty Papers, HCA 30/258.

CHAPTER X

Some Thumbnail Sketches

The following pen-pictures of some of the felons who were transported and came to notice through the notoriety of their offences, their appearance in court as the result of returning from transportation, or through appeals made on their behalf, will serve to illustrate the variety of their backgrounds, careers and experiences. Many eventually suffered the death penalty and, only by achieving this melancholy distinction, ensured that their biographies were ever written.

William Riddlesden, an attorney, was an accomplice of the notorious Jonathan Wild, "Thief-Taker Extraordinary," and was convicted of breaking into the Banqueting House in Whitehall and stealing plate from the communion table for which he was pardoned in August 1715 on condition that he transported himself for seven years. He set out for Maryland, but not before acquiring a large cargo of cutlery to set himself up in trade — and an elegant mistress. While residing in Annapolis in great splendour, he applied for, and was refused, an attorney's licence before being charged with forging one of his own. At this he returned to England and married the daughter of a wealthy merchant of Newcastle-upon-Tyne but, before he could lay his hands on her fortune, was once more thrown into Newgate, in April 1720, for having returned to the country before the expiry of his term of transportation. This man of many parts is probably to be identified with the William Vanhasdonk Riddlesdon on whose behalf his brother, Vanhelmont, on 21 April 1719, lodged an appeal claiming that William had been sentenced and transported for a capital offence on the accusation of a notorious criminal who was formerly a servant of the family. Because the petitioner and his brother, according to the petition, were heirs to a considerable estate left to them on the demise of a near relative, it had been necessary for William Riddlesdon to return in order to administer it.

At Riddlesden's insistence, an approach was made on his behalf to the Bank of England from whom he had expected support as a former colleague. The best the Bank's Board of Directors could manage on his behalf was a letter of 3 May 1723 declaring that, dangerous though Riddlesden was, and despite his return from transportation, they were unwilling to prosecute him. They suggested a *nolli prosequi* to be found on condition that Riddlesden transported himself again for seven years. So once more Riddlesden found himself obliged to go into exile, this time to Pennsylvania, where he set up as a tallow chandler, again applied for an attorney's licence and was again refused. In less than a year he was back in England running a public house in Golden Lane, London, before being arrested in Cambridge under the name of Cornwallis.[1]

John Meff, *alias* **Merth,** *alias* **Mason,** whose parents were refugees from the religious persecution in France under Louis XIV, was born in London and apprenticed to a weaver while his father, with the rest of the family, decamped to Holland to become a gardener in Amsterdam. Meff served his full time as an apprentice before marrying and attempting to support himself and his small child by honest work. Finding this an impossibility, he went into crime and was sentenced for housebreaking. On the way to the gallows, however, the hangman was put under arrest and Meff was brought back to Newgate where his sentence was commuted to transportation. He was embarked with other convicts but their ship was captured by pirates and all on board were offered the opportunity of serving under the skull and crossbones. Meff, and eight others who refused, were put ashore on a deserted and uninhabited island to die but, by extraordinary chance, a party of Indians arrived on the island in a canoe. As soon as the Indians moored their craft, the castaways seized it and sailed to the coast of America. Because of his great longing to see his wife and children again, Meff made his way from Virginia to South Carolina and from there to London where he was promptly arrested for returning from transportation and was hanged on 11 September 1721.[2]

William Barton of St. Pancras, Middlesex, was executed on 12 May 1721 for robbing John, Viscount Lisbon, and told his story while awaiting his last journey to the gallows. He was born in Thames Street, London, and raised by his grandfather, who kept an eating-house in Covent Garden, after his father had run off with a whore to Jamaica, leaving his wife and family to fend for themselves. Soon after his twelfth birthday, Barton ran away to sea and made his way to Jamaica where he found his father had died leaving his whole estate to his mistress. He took to the sea again, and after many adventures, returned to England to join the Army in the Flanders campaign. Upon his discharge he married but, finding it difficult to survive, took to thieving to support his wife and child. He was arrested, sentenced and transported by the *Worcester* in 1719 to Annapolis where he was sold to a planter for £18. He was employed in Maryland as an overseer of negroes and "to lash them when they neglected their work." He confessed that this was the happiest time of his life but, when he had completed all but a year of his sentence, the yearning for his wife overcame him, so he ran away and returned to his native land.[3]

Sir Charles Burton, Bt. of St. Gregory's, London, scion of a landed family in Lincolnshire, was indicted in 1722 for stealing a gold seal from a shop while he was in reduced circumstances. Though found guilty and ordered to be transported, at the following Sessions the order was commuted to a "private whipping."[4]

William Burk of St. Dunstan, Stepney, was the child of such poor parents that the only way he could receive any education was through a charity school at St. Katherine's-by-the-Tower, London. He persevered here until the age of eleven but then ran away to sea. Arriving eventually in the West Indies, he was taken into service by a rich widow who had formerly been an inmate of Newgate and had been transported for her crimes. She had married a rich planter who soon after died, since when she had occupied herself by running a tavern. Burk soon married her and set about relieving her of her money, but his new wife was too well versed in the arts of deception herself for the attempt to pass unnoticed, so Burk was obliged to take to the sea again. He moved to Maryland, became involved in the slave trade, plotted to seize the ship in which he served, failed, and returned to England where he again took up a seafaring career. At length he wearied of the sea and reverted to a life of crime which brought him to the gallows in February 1723 for a highway robbery.[5]

William Blewitt, hanged at Kingston, Surrey, in April 1726, was born in 1700 in Cripplegate, London, where his father was a porter and his mother kept a herb-stall. He was apprenticed to a perfumer of gloves but found the work tedious and took to a life of crime.

For the theft of a handkerchief he was sentenced in April 1722. No
sooner was he on board the ship *Alexander*, under Mr. John Graham,
bound for Nevis, than he contrived a plot to seize the ship by
smuggling on board files and saws concealed in cakes of gingerbread,
but, before his plan took effect, he betrayed his companions to the
captain. As a reward he was put ashore at Nevis as a free man. Very
soon returning to London, he was taken up in January 1724 on the
capital charge of having returned from transportation before the
expiration of his sentence. He made no denial but pointed instead to
the services he had rendered on board ship, thereby preventing the
escape of the other convicts and saving a valuable cargo. Jonathan
Forward, called in to testify on his behalf, acknowledged his services,
and Blewitt was thereby saved from the rope on condition that he
transported himself again to complete his sentence, and was listed
as an involuntary passenger to Virginia on the *Rappahannock Merchant* in December 1724. Immediately upon his arrival there, he
purchased his release and returned to England. Not long afterwards
he was implicated in the murder of Thomas Bell at the Mint,
Southwark. To avoid the hue and cry he fled to The Hague where,
by the vigilance of the resident British Minister, he was apprehended
and returned to London to hang.[6] A petition from him survives[7] in
which he says that, after being sentenced for stealing a handkerchief
to the value of ten pence, he was "instructed by merchant [Jonathan]
Forward in their voyage thither to take care of the rest of the fellons
[who] gott off all their handcuffs and Irons and were about to have
mutineyed in the said shipp and which was timely prevented by your
petitioner, and the lives of severall persons thereby saved." Blewitt
pleaded that his return from transportation was occasioned only by
the love of his wife and two small children (he was alleged to have
married several wives), "but with a pure design to have gone over
again and take them along with him."

James Dalton was born in St. Sepulchre's Parish, London, in about
1700, the son of a tailor of Dublin, Ireland, who was hanged at
Tyburn when his son was only five. His mother then married a
butcher before being arrested and transported for a felony. In 1730
she was "living in some of these foreign Places where she may have
leisure to lament the Fate of herself and her deserving Family; for
a sister of his [James Dalton's] is likewise transported." By the age
of eleven, he was already a member of a gang of thieves and whores.
He enjoyed a brief respite from their company when he joined the

British army and fought in Flanders where he was promoted to the rank of sergeant. On his discharge, he was first taken up for a robbery in Islington but escaped conviction by producing in court a number of his acquaintance who impersonated a doctor, apothecary and surgeon to swear that, at the relevant time, he had been in bed with a fever. But his continued life of crime soon brought him back before the justices, this time to be convicted and shipped on the *Honor* for the plantations. During a great storm at sea, Dalton and others were released from their irons to assist in saving the ship, but instead overpowered the crew and sailed her to Vigo in Spain. There Dalton and sixteen others procured a pass from the Governor but, finding that it described them as "English Thieves," consigned it to the flames and took a ship to Amsterdam. Dalton then removed himself to Bristol to continue his felonious career and was soon arrested for robbing a draper's shop. Transported again to Virginia in 1721 (by the *Prince Royal*) and sold to a planter, he was easily able to intimidate his master into giving him his freedom. He went, according to his own account, from place to place stealing ships and negroes and selling them with the assistance of a notorious robber named John Whalebone who had been transported to Virginia by the *Forward* in 1723). Tiring of this way of life, Dalton returned to his old haunts in London once more and, to save his skin when he was arrested in 1728 for yet more crimes, he turned King's evidence against six of his accomplices who were duly hanged. While awaiting execution, Dalton confessed that what most troubled his conscience was the number of widows and girls he had debauched. (The printed account alleges that he also married several wives in England, a number of whom were also transported, and left other wives in America.) At the last moment Dalton received a royal pardon and was discharged. His life thereafter remains unrecorded.[8]

Joseph Johnson, *alias* **Hodson,** hanged at Tyburn on 19 July 1738 at the age of forty-two, was born in the parish of St. Lawrence Jewry, London, the son of a porter. He acquired his education in the meaner streets around the London Guildhall before becoming a pickpocket. By 1720 he was in partnership with Dick Berry (later executed) and embarked on grander exploits for which he was clapped into Newgate and sentenced to be transported. While awaiting his ship, he became acquainted with an Irishman, also sentenced to transportation, who was in possession of a high denomination banknote which he had stolen. With the help of the ship's captain, both men were landed in

New York where they ran up debts amounting to £80 in the tavern where they lodged. The captain thereupon took possession of the banknote, paid off the landlord, gave the surplus in cash to Johnson and the Irishman, and sailed for Holland. The two accomplices then "travelled elegantly as squires" before Johnson returned to his native London. Meanwhile the captain had tendered the banknote in Rotterdam where it was discovered to have been stolen and was thrown into prison there until he could obtain written affidavits from New York to exculpate him. There is reason to suspect the infamous Jonathan Wild of having engineered Johnson's ultimate downfall since he had been heard to complain of Johnson's "locking," i.e. of selling goods outright to fences without consultation with Wild, thereby depriving the latter of the rewards offered by the original owners.[9]

Mary Young, *alias* **Murphew,** *alias* **Jane Webb,** *alias* **Jenny Diver**, was born in Northern Ireland of unknown parentage and was brought up and put to school by an old woman she knew simply as "Nurse." Having begun a career in crime by the age of ten, she sailed to England when she was fifteen to become a specialist in "Cheving the Froe," i.e. cutting women's pockets open, especially as they thronged to leave the London theatres. During her noviciate she was appointed as "Miss Slang upon the Safe," which required her, so as to appear an innocent bystander, to post herself at a distance from her gang while they picked pockets and to receive the stolen goods afterwards. She graduated with honours to become an accepted leader and acquired the name of Jenny Diver or Diving Jenny because of her dexterity as a pickpocket. She prevailed upon her gang to introduce the following rules:

> 1. No one to be admitted to the gang without the consent of all members.
>
> 2. No person to be permitted to embark on private thefts on pain of being dismissed.
>
> 3. Any proposed new member to serve a month's probation and, during that time, to be instructed in the "Cant Tongue," that is, to be able to speak intelligibly to members of the gang but to be incomprehensible to anyone else.
>
> 4. If any member was taken up, all the other members to swear to anything in order to secure a release but, if the member were convicted, an allowance to become payable to that member while in prison to enable him or her to live as a gentleman or gentlewoman.

In less than three years under her management, it was estimated that each member of the gang had acquired more than £300. Her career was briefly interrupted in April 1728 when she was convicted as a pickpocket and transported to the plantations by the *Elizabeth* under the name of Mary Webb. But she was soon back in London where she took to robbing society dames. In order to secure admission to the more fashionable houses, she went about the better quarters of London dressed as a lady and accompanied by her personal maid, having acquired residence in stylish lodgings in Covent Garden. In April 1738 she was detected in crime and again deported, this time under the name of Jane Webb, but her exile was even briefer than before. In January 1741 she was picked up near the Mansion House after an assault with violence, convicted, and executed on 18 March.[10]

Henry Cole, executed on 8 June 1744 for returning from transportation before the end of his term, was born of respectable parents in the parish of St. Dunstan-in-the-West, London. His mother died when he was young and, on the remarriage of his father, he was sent to sea and then bound apprentice to "an honest man in Maryland." He was later brought back to England to be trained as a sheriff's officer but fell into bad company and started a career of crime in partnership with a Margaret Dyer who lived with him as his wife. In 1738 both were convicted at the Surrey Sessions and were transported to Virginia to be sold to a Thomas Lewis. Margaret died ten days later and Henry remained racked with fever and ague for eight months before making his escape. He travelled through the country by night to reach Ockaquan, ten miles from his master's house, where he saw an advertisement pinned up outside a smithy offering a reward for his recapture. As he slowly made his way towards Rappahannock River and "was looking at one of the Country Posts which was set up with a Direction cut upon it, a woman came out to make water." Spotting Cole, she cried out to her husband that she had seen a runaway but, when the husband appeared with a gun, Cole gave him a false name and story. Though he was not satisfied with his story, he let Cole go, but almost at once he was again apprehended by "one Bryan, a planter in Virginia, an Irish fellow who had married an old Negroe Woman." He was hauled before a justice of the peace where a party of negroes pleaded for him: "Poor Barricado, let him go; what signifies keeping him?" The justice was all for throwing Cole into jail until his master should reclaim him, but Cole managed to persuade him that he was on the run merely to escape a debt, for "if a man cannot

pay his debts, they will sell him for a slave till those debts are paid."
On his release he wandered on until he was press-ganged into H.M.S.
Scarborough. In September 1740 he again made his escape in order
to resume his former life of crime in England.[11]

Joseph Lewin of West Ham, Middlesex, was executed on 21
October 1743 at the age of twenty-seven for returning from transportation (having gone by the *Essex* in June 1740 to serve a term of
seven years). He was born of honest, poor parents who gave him a
good education and then apprenticed him to a calico printer. Despite
this background, he was badly behaved from his youth and associated
with gangs of thieves, pickpockets and loose women. Averse to all
industry and the idea of work, he was first confined in Newgate on
a charge of stealing from his master, after which he went into Essex
where he stole cloth for which he was sentenced to be transported
to Maryland. There he was bought by a very rigid and severe master
who beat him cruelly and unmercifully. But a Pennsylvania widow
took pity on him, purchased his services, and offered him such kind
treatment that he was persuaded to marry her. The widow's eight
children were incensed that their mother should have taken a transported thief to husband and given him land and slaves. When she gave
him money to buy clothes in Philadelphia, he reverted to form and
squandered it all on drink and debauchery before embarking on a ship
bound for New England and Leith, Scotland. He made the mistake of
going to London to visit his poor old father, was recognised as a returned
transport and arrested. While in prison he was visited by a poor young
woman who claimed to be his wife and to have had three children
by him. Joseph at first denied knowledge of a previous marriage but
(no doubt influenced by the imminence of a gallows death) finally
confessed: "I was married to several wives, what does it signify?"[12]

Samuel Ellard, hanged at Tyburn on 7 November 1744, was born
in 1714 to honest parents in Spitalfields, his father being a master
weaver. He received a short schooling until his father died and was
then apprenticed to a butcher with whom he served his full time.
Once freed, he worked in Spitalfields Market and was of generally
good character until he was tempted to steal money. For this he was
transported by the *Catherine and Elizabeth* to Maryland in 1741 and
sold to a planter "who used him very cruel . . . his Master being a
Grecian of most savage disposition [and] whipp'd seven of his Men
to Death; and his Master's Wife, who was an Irishwoman, being
likewise of a turbulent spirit, he was determined if possible to run

away [and] filling his pockets with what Victuals he could find, set out in the Evening after he had done work, travelled all that night and next day, and so on until he reached Philadelphia which was above 300 miles distant from his Master's Plantation." On his journey he was arrested several times on suspicion of being a runaway since he had no pass, but "the people pitied him, turned him loose and gave him Victuals." He returned to London in 1742 to work again, rather unwisely, in the market where, "although several people knew of his misfortune, none offered to molest him." He married a year later but was then arrested in the parish of St. Martin Ludgate and condemned to die for having returned from transportation. He left a wife in the final stages of pregnancy.[13]

Joseph Lucas, born in the parish of St. Luke's, London, was apprenticed to a flaxter but deserted him in favour of thieving and, before he reached the age of fifteen, had committed several robberies. In Virginia, where he was sent (by the *Patapsco Merchant* in 1735) to repent, he was "in a tolerable way of living," and married a wife who was also a transport. They stayed together for ten years in Virginia but then agreed to return to England, "not finding any opportunity where they were of exerting themselves to any purpose." Lucas returned to his life of crime for which he was condemned to the gallows. Just before his execution in 1745, he wrote to his wife:

> All the vanities and follies of this world are now no more . . . There may be some hopes of a reprieve but, for my part, it is the least of my thoughts; for however miserable the world may think me now, I am really happier than ever. I have no way to prove this to you but by wishing you to try how pleasurable it is to have honest thoughts: you know very well that, ever since our return from Virginia, we have had neither rest nor peace; now I have both and am satisfied. Then we feared death as the greatest evil, now I embrace it as the greatest good, and am more afraid of having a reprieve to live again and be miserable, than I used to be of Justice De Veil and his Constables. It is a sad thing to be always in fear, it is living a dog's life: for the Lord's sake find some way to live honestly if it is but by keeping a chandler's shop. You need not be told the danger of receiving stolen goods when it puts you in the power of every little pilfering rascal to ruin you whenever he pleases; they durst not do it whilst I was alive, but now I am dead they will hang you if they can to save themselves. Only consider what became of Bess Cane [*see below*]. Bess is gone to be a slave and you know what that

is; don't go there any more, my heart bleeds to think on't . . . Adieu, my Dear; the bell tolls, I am going to heaven I hope, where I shall rejoice to embrace you . . ."[14]

Elizabeth Cane, *alias* **Lawrence,** was tried before the Middlesex justices in December 1744 for receiving stolen goods, was found guilty and sentenced to be transported for fourteen years. She arrived in Maryland in October 1745 and, by her own account, was first sold to a planter and then purchased from him by her brother and shipped to his home in Boston. But, while at sea, her ship was taken by a French privateer. Bess and the other captives on board rose up a few days afterwards, overpowered the French crew, and sailed on into Boston. Upon her arrival there, she found that her brother had died leaving her enough money to lead an independent life. She made the almost fatal mistake of booking herself a passage back to England where she was arrested, tried and sentenced to death for returning from transportation before the expiration of her term. Upon an appeal from her native parish of St. Andrew's, Holborn, London, her sentence was commuted to a further term of transportation.[15]

George Hatcher (or Hatchett) was the son of a shoemaker in the parish of St. Margaret, Westminster, and, being left an orphan in 1722, was maintained first by a parish nurse and then put into the Greycoat Hospital from which he was bound apprentice to a black-smith in 1732. He quickly abandoned this onerous way of life in favour of thieving, was arrested in 1738 and transported for seven years to Virginia by the *Dorsetshire* in January 1739. He was sold as a blacksmith in King George County and, on the death of his master in 1744, was sold as part of his estate to Charles Ewell who shortly afterwards moved to Prince William County. Hatcher's fate came to light in 1745 only because an advertisement was placed in the papers for any son or grandson of Thomas Hatcher of Cheriton, Hampshire, to come forward to claim his estate consisting of a brewhouse and barn in Cheriton Manor. George Hatcher was shown to be a legitimate grandson.[16]

Henry Simms, executed for highway robbery in 1746, was born in the parish of St. Martin's-in-the-Fields. He lost his father when he was young and was brought up by his grandmother, a dissenter. He was apprehended after robbing a baker's shop and was sentenced to be transported in May 1745. He hatched a plot to seize the transport ship off the Isle of Wight but, because of the strict watch kept upon him, the attempt failed. He was sold for twelve guineas in Maryland and, soon afterwards, stole his master's horse on which, he boasted, he covered thirty miles in four hours over extremely bad roads. He found himself by the seaside and, turning the horse loose, he hailed a vessel just under sail (the *Two Sisters*, under Mr. James Abercrombie) from which a boat was sent to bring him on board. As hands were very scarce, the captain offered him six guineas to work his passage to England, but their ship was captured by a French privateer and taken into Oporto. There Simms joined the *King's Fisher* in order to reach Falmouth from where he travelled back to London to resume his former activities.[17]

John Harvey, a farmer of Pond Hall, Suffolk, was condemned to death for being at large in England before the expiry of his term of transportation and confined at Great Yarmouth to await execution. His appeal relates that he was originally sentenced for smuggling at the Old Bailey in October 1747. On the passage to America his ship was seized by a Spanish privateer and he was taken to Spain, exchanged by cartel, and then taken to Jamaica. From there he shipped back to England to join his wife and seven children who were "quite destitute of bread."[18]

William Curtis, finding himself imprisoned in Bristol in 1739, had acted as a hangman on his own initiative (no doubt in order to mitigate his own sentence), but only a few months later was himself sentenced to death at the Gloucester Assizes for robbing a Scottish pedlar. He was pardoned in 1740 on condition that he served a fourteen-year sentence of transportation but in less than a year was back in Bristol. There he discovered the same Scottish pedlar, whom he regarded as the cause of his woes, locked up in a debtors' prison. Curtis visited the prison each day to heap insults and curses on the pedlar who was finally driven to denounce him with the result that Curtis was hanged in April 1747 for having returned to England before the expiry of his sentence.[19]

William, *alias* **Richard, Parsons** was executed at Tyburn on 11 February 1751 for returning from transportation. He was the son of Sir William Parsons who impoverished himself in support of the Pretender. By the age of fourteen, when he was at Eton School, young Parsons had earned himself the sobriquet of Robbing Parsons because of his thieving ways, and in 1735 had to be taken away. He was entered into the Navy as a midshipman which gave him scope for many amorous adventures and, having risen to the rank of Lieutenant, he married a wealthy heiress whose friends saw to it that her full fortune was withheld on account of her husband's reputation. Parsons had one son by this marriage but used his wife very badly and, on one occasion, when she was away visiting, he sold all her goods which he could lay hands on. After a long series of swindles, he was arrested for forgery and sentenced to death at Rochester, Kent, in 1749 but was reprieved on condition of transportation. While awaiting a ship, he was detained in a cell which he shared with a Thomas Rogers, also sentenced to transportation. Learning that Rogers intended to take his life savings of £40 with him to America, Parsons quickly relieved him of the greater part, which he used to purchase a passage for himself in the steerage of the *Thames* "and not among the common people." He took with him into exile a large chest of clothes, and arrangements were made for him to draw an allowance of £30 a year in America. He behaved well on shipboard, befriending Captain James Dobbins to such good effect that he was allowed the free use of the captain's cabin. Once in Annapolis he took up his lodgings in the Duke's Head to await his removal to more agreeable surroundings, "for as all persons who are transported, though they agree with the Merchant for their freedom when there, yet they are known to be Transports and so consequently are looked on in a scandalous manner." When Parsons began to spread scurrilous accounts of the way Captain Dobbins had treated his cargo of felons, the captain sought him out and thrashed him with his cane, "at first imagining that a sufficient reproof to one so much beneath a man of any honour." However, Parsons pursued his allegations and took Dobbins before a local magistrate only to be rebuked for such monstrously false charges. During his brief stay in Annapolis, Parsons found time to swindle a merchant out of £70 by pretending that his father had died in England and that he needed to return there to take possession of a large estate. A former acquaintance introduced Parsons to the Governor of Virginia, Lord Fairfax, who took a liking to him and invited him to stay at his house. Parsons rewarded him by breaking open a cabinet, stealing money and a horse, and then fleeing. "The country beginning to be too hot to tarry in," he then swindled another merchant of the price of his return ticket and took ship to Whitehaven, Cumberland, where he resumed his old career.[20]

Elizabeth Canning was indicted in May 1754 for perjury in saying she had been robbed. Some 50,000 wagers were said to have been made on the outcome of her trial at which she was found guilty and sentenced to be transported to New England in July 1754, having first received £100 donated by her friends and partisans of her cause. She was reputed to have married a John Treat in 1756 and to have died at Wethersfield, Connecticut, on 22 July 1773, an event which was reported in the English papers.[21]

Francis Smith, who was hanged on 12 October 1763 for returning from transportation, confessed on the eve of his execution that his real name was Isaac Hawes and that he was born in Red Lion Street, Holborn, London, the son of a clog-maker, to which business he was brought up until he went to sea at the age of sixteen. Under his real name he was sentenced in April 1753 to be transported and was shipped to Maryland by the *Thames* and served his full term of seven years before returning home to resume a career of thieving. He was arrested again in 1760 but, because of the great need there then was for army recruits, he was allowed to enlist in the 49th Regiment to go to Jamaica, broke out of the barracks, was captured, forcibly embarked on board the transport ship, and then contrived to escape again. He made his way to Coventry where he joined the local gang of thieves under the name of Sherwood. In April 1762 he was once more arrested and sentenced to be transported by the *Neptune*. This time he hid behind the coach which was conveying two other felons to the ship, unhitched it and caused it to overturn, and then escaped in the confusion. A year later he was seen again in London plying his old occupation from Tower Hill to the Strand. When he was arrested for the last time to stand trial, he claimed mistaken identity, alleging that in August 1762 he had been press-ganged at Yorktown, Virginia, for H.M.S. *Jason*, this time under the name of Alexander Brown, and was able to produce a certificate from the captain of that ship. Unfortunately for him, both the captain's name and that of his ship had been wrongly spelled, and a check of the ship's books soon revealed that the prisoner had never enlisted on it.[22]

William Green, whose own account of his trial and deportation survives in print,[23] was born at Mansfield, Nottinghamshire, on 4 June 1748, and at the age of seven was taken to London by his parents to be entered into a free school at London Bridge for seven years until he was ready to be apprenticed to a weaver at Shoreditch. He immediately fell into the hands of a gang with whom he ran away to Sherwood Forest to follow in the tradition of Robin Hood. Just turned fifteen, he was betrayed by one of the gang who hoped to save his own skin, sentenced to transportation and shipped to Maryland. After a six-weeks' passage during which he appears to have been reasonably well treated, he was sold by the ship's captain to a planter who stripped him of his good clothes and put him into "lousy rags." For five years he was obliged to work in the fields, six days of the week for his master and one day in order to provide food for himself. With only two years of his servitude left, he was sold to the master of a New England schooner with whom he went whaling and much enjoyed the experience. He managed to save £20 with which he paid his own and a friend's return passage to England. He took the stage from Dover to London where he was able to trace his father and mother living in Highgate: they had not heard of him for over seven years. Green wrote an account of his sufferings to point out "the dreadful effects of breaking the well-regulated and established laws of our country" and closed his narrative with a warning to others who might be tempted into a life of crime: "Be assured that like horses you must slave, and like galley-slaves you will be used."

Richard Swift, the son of poor parents in Old Street, London, received some education before being apprenticed to a turner. Though he was many times committed to Newgate on suspicion of crime, he was always acquitted until, when he was nearly fifty, he was convicted in June 1764 of receiving stolen candles and sentenced to be transported for fourteen years. He had not been in America more than a month before he shipped back to Liverpool. While making his way back to London he was recognised and arrested in Coventry but released on a technicality. But as soon as he reached London he was re-arrested and put on board a transport ship for a second time in April 1765.[24]

Robert Jones was convicted for sodomy in July 1772 and pardoned on condition that he transported himself. "He quitted Newgate privately," wrote his biographer, "and embarked for some foreign shore. What became of him afterwards we have never learnt, nor can the reader be solicitous to know."[25]

NOTES

1. PRO (Public Record Office): State Papers Criminal, SP 44/251/280, 253/278, 257/285; notes in *Tyburn Chronicle* (1768), Vol. II.

2. *Tyburn Chronicle*, Vol. I.

3. *Select Trials at the Old Bailey* (London, 1742), Vol. I.

4. *Select Trials*, Vol. I; *Malefactors' Register* (London, 1779), Vol. III.

5. *Select Trials*, Vol. I.

6. *Malefactors' Register*, Vol. II; *Tyburn Chronicle*, Vol. II.

7. PRO: State Papers, SP 36/150. The treatment accorded to an informer by his erstwhile comrades has changed little over the years. Edward Lyons, who turned informer in 1725 in order to avoid a death sentence, was instrumental in bringing several felons to justice. He afterwards complained: "As soon as I am gotten into a place of work they call me nothing but an informer, and even going along a street, people do the same, and the noise of my being confined obliged my poor distressed family to break up what small settlement they had." (PRO: SP 36/154.)

8. *Select Trials*, Vol. III.

9. Old Bailey Sessions Papers for 1738.

10. *Select Trials*, Vol. IV.

11. Old Bailey Sessions Papers for 1743; *Tyburn Chronicle*, Vol. IV.

12. Old Bailey Sessions Papers for 1743.

13. *Ibid.*, for 1744.

14. *Ibid.*, for 1745.

15. PRO: State Papers, SP 36/154.

16. PRO: Chancery Bill, Answers and Depositions in *Avenell* v. *Hickman*, C11/448/8 and C24/1588/26, 1745.

17. *Tyburn Chronicle*, Vol. III.

18. PRO: State Papers, SP 36/150.

19. John Latimer, *op. cit.*, p. 237.

20. *Tyburn Chronicle*, Vol. IV.

21. *Malefactors' Register*, Vol. IV.

22. Old Bailey Sessions Papers for October 1763.

23. William Green, *op. cit.*

24. *Malefactors' Register*, Vol. IV.

25. *Ibid.*, Vol. V.

CHAPTER XI

The Twilight Years

The last convict ship reported as arriving in America was the *Jenny* from Newcastle, which put its passengers ashore from the James River in April 1776.[1] The complete cessation of the white slave trade to America can be determined with accuracy from a further letter written by Campbell to the Treasury on 11 December 1776 with which he enclosed a report on the convicts received aboard his ship *Tayloe* for transportation but who were subsequently discharged with a pardon on condition that they entered the armed forces. It is for speculation whether this contingent, originally cast for work in the American plantations, eventually found themselves in the same part of the world but as soldiers in George III's army. Campbell's letter concluded:

> As to what you are pleased to direct for making proposals for the future maintenance of these Felons . . . all the Gaols now being cleared of the Felons for transportation, and that as soon as the sickness was over, which for some time past has prevailed on board to a greater degree than I have ever known, there would be no further service for the ship [the *Tayloe*]; that this business will then be finely [i.e. finally] closed; and as the few people remaining on board will then, I have no doubt, in a few days be in a Healthy state, it may be unnecessary for me to trouble Their Lordships at this time with any further proposals on that score.[2]

An effective alternative to transportation had to be found quickly, not only to rid the prisons of an intolerably swollen population but to restore to the judges the intimidatory power of a penalty now deeply grafted into the judicial system. The Lord Mayor of London, having voiced in November 1775 "uneasiness at the long detention of the Transport Convicts in Newgate, and being very apprehensive of the Prison becoming dangerous to the Lives of all who are confined in it, or may attend the Old Bailey," the Home Office proposed to Duncan Campbell that he should immediately take all those condemned to transportation into one of his ships on the River Thames "in the usual manner and as if in due Course for Transportation."[3] A scheme was devised to divert criminal labour to river and harbour works in England until, as was confidently anticipated, the American market reopened. The convicts were to be accommodated in rotting hulks along the River Thames and elsewhere. To legalise this new arrangement the so-called Hulk Act was pushed through in 1776. Its preamble refers with some delicacy to the fact that "transportation of convicts to America is found to be attended by various inconveniences." Many of the hulks used were ships taken from the transportation trade, and Duncan Campbell was recompensed for his previous services by being appointed Superintendent of the Thames Area, in which capacity he became responsible for 510 male convicts. The civil administrators found the Act a poor substitute for transportation as is evident from the following notes by a Middlesex justice:

> The Hulk Act has been very burdensome to Middlesex on account of the great number of criminals. By that Act female criminals, many of whom were formerly transported, old men, boys, etc., who could not properly be sent to hard labours on the Thames, were imprisoned. This has obliged the County since the Hulk Act to spend £2000 in fitting up proper places for the reception of such criminals tho' the County had a very few years before spent nearly £5000 in enlarging and strengthening their gaols. Up to now £50 per annum has been paid to the Surgeon for attending the gaols, but since the Hulk Act the County has been obliged to pay him £100 per annum. A further allowance of £50 per annum has also had to be paid to the Keeper of Clerkenwell and Bridewell. The maintenance of convicts costs 3 pence per head a day and comes to £300-£400 a year. No profit has been got from the labour of the convicts . . . The idea of obliging the poor industrious Housekeeper, oppressed with taxes, to contribute under the name of a Poor Tax to support the felon who has robbed him is almost repugnant to Humanity.[4]

From the first, the Hulk Act was perceived as merely a temporary expedient forced upon the administration during a period of exceptional difficulty. Old traditions and habits of thought died hard: North America had for so long been thought of as the natural dumping ground for unwanted felons that preparations were already afoot to resume transportation on the former pattern when the humiliating Peace Treaty of 1783 was signed. Accordingly, Lord North wrote to the Governor of Nova Scotia on 12 August 1783 to inform him that arrangements had been made with a shipowner named George Moore to take 150 felons there who were to be allowed to land "as hath been used on former occasions." Most of the felons making up this consignment were to be taken from the Thames hulks while a fresh draft of eighty-seven came from Newgate Prison. But this was all a clumsy and ill-starred stratagem devised with the connivance of the British Government to reintroduce convict transportation in its old form. Moore agreed with George Salmon, a merchant in Baltimore, to send his ship *George* under the assumed name of the *Swift* ostensibly to Nova Scotia but in fact to Maryland, and to conceal the true identity of her passengers by describing them as indentured servants. On 17 August the *Swift* under Captain Thomas Pamp sailed from London with 143 convicts on board. Within two weeks of his departure, he had cause to regret the humane treatment he had allowed his charges by bringing them on deck without fetters twenty at a time for exercise and relief from the fetid conditions below. During their temporary freedom, the felons contrived to unchain their companions until there were enough at liberty to overpower the crew and take over the ship. The command was given to a convict with some previous seafaring experience, Peter Duncan, but his qualities were not such as to impress his comrades, forty-eight of whom decided to make off in the ship's long boat to the southern shore of England. The ninety-five convicts remaining on board then decided that their interests lay in releasing the regular crew but, when the mutineers turned to drink, the seamen recaptured the *Swift* and sailed her into Portsmouth escorted by H.M.S. *Perseverance*. Meanwhile a hue and cry had been sent out for those who had formerly escaped and who were rampaging through the countryside on their way back to London. An outraged administration determined that exemplary punishment should be meted out. While the felons who had chosen to remain on board the *Swift* awaited their fate in Portsmouth, those who were captured in London or on their way were either hanged or put back in the hulks to serve the full term of their original sentences. The *Swift* then tried again. On 3 October 1783 she sailed with a new cargo of felons for Baltimore where she arrived on 24 December. Despite the fact that the authorities were by now fully aware of the hoax and had obdurately refused to renew the convict trade, eighty-seven felons from the *Swift* are noted in Maryland records as having been landed, though the list includes names of several already hanged in London and fails to mention sixty-six others known to have been embarked! By the spring of 1784 all but a handful had been sold on credit and, although many of the American buyers refused to honour their debts, Moore at least received the £500 he had been promised by the Treasury for engineering this venture.

By the beginning of 1784 the pressure on prison and hulk space decided the Government to test the American market again, and George Moore was asked to prepare another ship, the *Mercury*. In March fifty prisoners from the hulks, 105 from Newgate, and thirty from Maidstone and Oxford Jails (including a girl aged thirteen and two boys aged nine and eleven) were embarked for delivery to Georgia. The ship was struck by a storm and had to put into Torbay in April when it was discovered that yet again the convicts had commandeered the vessel, and this time well over a hundred had escaped. H.M.S. *Helena* recaptured sixty-six of them, another forty or more scattered through the western counties of England, and a few were picked up in London. Repaired and restored to her previous command, the *Mercury* received new orders to sail for Baltimore following information received by George Moore that the American States would be glad to receive her passengers. But, according to evidence given to a House of Commons committee later, "We tried it a second time and they would not receive them." The *Mercury's* orders were changed in such quick succession thereafter that no one could be certain what her final destination would be. She was instructed to sail first to Honduras, then to Virginia, and finally to Nova Scotia. In the event, she made port in Honduras in July 1784 where her passengers were landed, rejected, and taken back on board. Having now nowhere else to go, the ship remained in Honduras until October, by which time the convicts had taken matters into their own hands and scattered into the colony to be joined there by another shipload sent out by Moore in the *Fair American*.[5]

These dismal experiments seem finally to have convinced the Government that America should be written off as a vent for the country's prison population, though the legislators retained an almost nostalgic memory of the workings of the old system of transportation. In contrast, the American Congress, on 16 September 1788, resolved that the States should pass laws preventing the transportation of convicted malefactors from foreign counties, and the Virginia Act of

13 November 1788, passed in compliance with this resolution, forbade the importation of felons "whereby much injury hath been done to the morals as well as the health of our fellow citizens."

English administrators, however, found little complaint against the system of transportation when it came to be reviewed by a Parliamentary committee in 1785. The committee found that "it answered every good purpose that could be expected of it," for in addition to reclaiming prisoners and turning them into good citizens, "it was not attended with very much expense to the public, the convicts being carried out in vessels employed in the Jamaica and tobacco trade, the contractor being indemnified by the price at which he sold their labour."[6] Lord Ellenborough, Lord Chief Justice of England some years later, was moved to remember the practice of transportation as "a Summer's excursion in an easy migration to a happier and better climate."[7]

One hundred and fifty years' experience in the administration and management of transportation schemes was not, however, to be wasted. In May 1787 the first of many fleets, this one carrying 778 felons, left England to establish the new penal colonies in New South Wales.

How did expert opinion in England, after 150 years' experience of the benefits and problems of the system of penal transportation, view its record? Though its defenders viewed it as an effective method of eliminating undesirable and dangerous elements, Jeremy Bentham, the legal giant of his day, was quick to point out the many limitations of the practice of transportation as it affected young offenders who had no family ties or regular employment. His final verdict read:

> Among the advantages the North Americans have gained from their independence, there is one which cannot fail to strike every man who has any feeling of national pride: it has saved them from the humiliating obligation of receiving each year an importation of the refuse of the British population; of serving as an outlet for the prisons of the mother country, whereby the morals of their rising people were exposed to injury by a mixture of all possible kinds of depravity. North America, having been exposed to this scourge for upwards of a century, no longer serves as a receptacle for these living nuisances: but can any limit be assigned to the moral effects that may have been produced by this early inoculation of vice?

Whenever it happened that, through the medium of a friend or otherwise, the convict could bid more for himself than would be given for his services by a stranger, he was set at liberty in the first port in which he arrived . . . Thus the most culpable — those who had committed great crimes, and who had contrived to secure the profits of their crimes —were least punished. The minor thieves, novices and inexperienced malefactors, who had not secured their plunder, bore the double chain of banishment and slavery.

Transportation [is] eminently defective, particularly in respect of its inequality; hard labour, a punishment in itself eminently salutary but, when connected with banishment and . . . carried on under every possible disadvantage, failing altogether to produce any beneficial effects.

Bentham believed, however, that

There were two circumstances highly conducive to the reformation of the convicts transported [to America]. Their admission . . . into families composed of men of thrift and probity; their separation from each other. When a master in America had engaged a convict in his service, all the members of the family became interested in watching his behaviour [and] he had neither the inducements nor the means of giving loose to his vicious propensities . . .

He concluded:

The punishment of transportation . . . designed as a comparatively lenient punishment . . . is frequently converted into capital punishment. This . . . aggravation will be found to fall almost exclusively upon the least robust and least noxious class of offenders — those who, by their sensibility, former habits of life, sex and age — are least able to contend against the terrible visitation to which they are exposed during the course of a long and perilous voyage.[8]

NOTES

1. *Virginia Gazette* (25 April 1776).

2. PRO (Public Record Office): Treasury Papers, T1/521.

3. PRO: State Papers Criminal, SP 44/91. Hopes persisted in the face of all obstacles that the old system of transportation would soon return, as is clear from the fact that, as late as October 1776, thirty-two convicts were reported as having been held aboard a ship in the Thames for six months under sentence of transportation without knowing their destination. They then made their escape. See *Gentleman's Magazine*, Vol. 46 (1776), p. 480.

4. Middlesex Sessions Book for 1778.

5. This account is based on notes kindly provided by Mollie Gillen, author of several authoritative works on emigration to Australia. Further details are included in Wilfred Oldham, *Britain's Convicts to the Colonies*, Library of Australian History (Sydney, N.S.W., 1990), pp. 85-92, and A. R. Ekirch, "Great Britain's Secret Convict Trade to America 1783-1784," *American Historical Review*, Vol. 89 (1984), No. 5.

6. *House of Commons Reports*, Vol. 6, col. 61a and Vol. 7, col. 71.

7. *Parliamentary Debates* (1810), Vol. 17, col. 200.

8. Sir John Bowring, *Works of Jeremy Bentham* (Edinburgh, 1843), Vol. 1, pp. 403, 490-496.

Appendix I

PARDONS ON CONDITION OF TRANSPORTATION
(Patent Rolls: PRO series C66)

Year	Circuits						
	Newgate	Home	Western	Oxford	Norfolk	Northern, Flint & Chester	Midland
1655		2912/3					
1656	2912/7	2912/2					
1661	2986/1						
1662	3011/5	3011/14					
1663	3048/15 3049/14	3049/16 3048/12		3048/8, 16 3049/21	3048/10		
1664	3066/12, 13 3071/2, 3	3066/17 3071/10	3066/21	3066/23 3071/15	3071/13, 15 3066/10		
1665	3066/5 3073/20 3074/10, 99	3074/95	3073/25 3074/94, 100	3073/24	3066/8 3073/24	3066/6	
1666			3086/17	3086/3, 16		3086/2, 14	
1667	3088/4		3091/5				
1668	3098/11 3101/6, 19 3102/3	3101/6, 20, 22	3098/2 3101/18	3101/11 3102/2			
1669	3107/41, 47	3107/45	3107/48				
1670	(LRO copy)						
1671	3128/21	3128/17	3128/13, 41	3128/1, 42	3128/9	3128/2, 10	3128/39
1672	3137/2, 17		3137/12, 25		3137/6	3137/5	
1673	3145/2 3148/17		3145/6 3148/20	3148/5, 19		3148/18	3148/4
1674	3167/1	3167/2	3166/1				3167/3
1675	3170/38 3173/3	3173/23		3174/17	3174/16	3173/22	
1676	(LRO copy)	3187/24	3178/15			3186/11	
1677	3188/6 3200/15	3200/17	3200/21	3200/24		3200/22, 23	3200/25
1678	3204/7	3204/10, 14	3206/20	3204/9		3204/5	3204/13
1679	3205/31 3208/4 3214/25	3214/13	3210/2 3214/10	3214/17	3210/3	3210/6 3214/7	3214/16
1680	(LRO copy)	3216/32 3218/16		3217/6	3216/33		3219/6
1681	3222/17 3225/7		3223/4	3219/11 3223/1	3219/7	3223/5	3222/20
1682	3229/4	3228/2	3224/12	3229/1 3230/11	3228/14	3228/15 3229/2	3228/1, 10
1683	3235/30 3236/12	3235/36	3235/37 3239/27	3235/31 3239/20	3239/26	3239/25, 30	3235/38 3239/24
1684	3245/16	3245/13, 18	3245/11, 19	3245/14	3245/12	3245/15	3245/17
1685	3275/2 3276/12					3276/6	3276/1

159

Emigrants in Chains

Year	Newgate	Home	Western	Oxford	Norfolk	Northern, Flint & Chester	Midland
1686	3282/10 3288/20	3282/7	3282/6 3288/21 3290/11	3282/14 3287/7	3282/5	3288/25	3288/28
1687	3291/11 3297/16	3296/4	3296/1	3291/14 3296/2	3291/9	3297/11	3297/23
1688	3301/1 3309/1	3302/6 3305/8	3302/9 3303/11 3304/25 3305/14	3302/8 3304/25 3305/11	3302/10 3303/12	3305/9	3305/13
1689	3332/5						
1690	3335/9 3338/4, 12	3337/16	3334/21	3335/17 3339/3		3337/1	
1691	3345/2	3345/4	3339/1 3340/7	3334/3 3345/5	3345/6	3345/3	3340/6
1692	3348/11	3353/12	3349/12	3353/16		3353/13	3349/15
1693	3356/11 3360/15		3359/11 3365/7	3365/5	3359/5 3365/6		3365/8
1694	3375/11, 12	3369/20	3369/21	3375/2		3369/19 3370/12	3371/10
1695	3381/14	3380/15	3378/13 3380/9		3380/13		
1696	3381/2	3384/7	3384/11	3384/6		3385/18	3385/19T
1697	3390/13		3393/19	3393/16	3391/3 3393/13	3393/20	3393/14
1698	3398/12	3403/11	3403/15 3405/8	3405/3	3403/9	3403/8 3405/7	
1699	3411/16	3413/16	3412/16 3413/17	3412/14 3413/13		3412/7 3413/8, 14	3412/13
1700	3416/5	3416/7	3416/13 3417/27		3416/8	3416/4	3417/25
1701	3420/3		3419/29	3420/15		3419/14	
1702	3429/21	3429/33	3426/13 3429/8	3429/31	3426/9		3426/10
1703			3440/9		3440/2		
1704	3445/5	3444/17	3444/12	3438/6			3444/10
1705		3452/D8				3452/D7	
1706	3452/4 3454/10						3456/8
1707		3461/17		3461/16			3460/5
1708			3465/7				3465/6
1709	3468/4	3468/12		3465/5			3469/7
1710	3474/D2	3475/3	3472/2	3473/19	3472/1	3478/2	3472/5
1711			3484/20	3482/8		3482/5	3482/7
1712	3488/1	3488/2					
1713	3493/3			3486/9	3490/15		3486/10
1714		3497/12	3494/9	3494/6 3497/11	3497/6		3497/14
1715	3512/27	3507/12	3508/21			3507/13	
1716	3519/10		3516/4	3513/4			3516/5
1717			3520/4	3520/20			
1718							3523/12
1719		3530/1		3530/7		3530/6	

Appendix II

SUMMARY LIST OF PRINCIPAL GAOL
DELIVERY AND ASSIZE RECORDS

The majority of those felons transported between 1718 and 1775 were sentenced at Sessions of Gaol Delivery held separately for the City of London, for Middlesex, and for each of the circuits into which the other counties of England were arranged. The principal means of reference are as follows:

City of London

Records held by the Corporation of London Record Office, P.O. Box 270, Guildhall, London EC2P 2EJ.

Sessions Minute Books, arranged in annual volumes, briefly record the names of prisoners and the sentences imposed.

Sessions Rolls, one for each session of the court, include indictments for each prisoner, giving his name, quality, details of his offence, and a superscribed note of sentence.

Transportation Bonds 1718-1772. Originals of the bonds which transportation contractors and ships' captains signed with London justices to ensure the effective shipment to the colonies of named convicts.

Landing Certificates 1718-1736. Certificates signed by customs officers at the convicts' port of arrival recording the names of those safely landed.

Middlesex

Records held by the Greater London Record Office, 40 Northampton Road, London EC1 0AB.

Gaol Delivery Registers 1620-1672. Six large registers recording the names of prisoners arraigned with periodic lists showing those pardoned on condition of transportation.

161

Gaol Delivery Books. Similar in content to the *Sessions Minute Books* above. From 1718 to 1733 and from 1738 to 1756 the Books contain copies of transportation bonds with contractors.

Gaol Delivery Sessions Rolls. In the same form as *Sessions Rolls* listed above.

Transportation Bonds 1720-1756 and 1771-1775. *As above.*

Assize Circuits

Most other Assize and Gaol Delivery records are housed at the Public Record Office, Chancery Lane, London WC2A 1LR, as follows:

Home Circuit, comprising the counties of Essex, Hertfordshire, Kent, Surrey and Sussex.

Gaol Delivery Rolls: ASSI 35.

Western Circuit, comprising the counties of Cornwall, Devon, Dorset, Hampshire, Somerset and Wiltshire.

Gaol Books: ASSI 23.

Order Books: ASSI 24.

Crown Minute Books: ASSI 21.

Oxford Circuit, comprising the counties of Berkshire, Gloucestershire, Herefordshire, Monmouthshire, Oxfordshire, Shropshire, Staffordshire and Worcestershire.

Gaol Delivery Rolls: ASSI 5.

Crown Minute Books: ASSI 2.

Norfolk Circuit, comprising the counties of Bedfordshire, Buckinghamshire, Cambridgeshire, Huntingdonshire, Norfolk and Suffolk.

Gaol Delivery Rolls: ASSI 16.

Gaol Books: ASSI 33/1, 34/17, 33/2-5 (also one volume now held by Gray's Inn Library as MS45).

Indictment Rolls: ASSI 35.

Northern Circuit, comprising the counties of Cumberland, Northumberland, Westmorland and Yorkshire.

Crown Minute Books: ASSI 41.

Gaol Books: ASSI 42.

Indictment Rolls: ASSI 44.

Midland Circuit, comprising the counties of Derbyshire, Leicestershire, Lincolnshire, Northamptonshire, Nottinghamshire, Rutland and Warwickshire. The documents of this circuit prior to 1800 were destroyed, and the names of those sentenced to transportation after 1718 need to be retrieved from alternative sources, principally:

Sheriffs' Cravings: E 370.

Domestic Papers: SP 35, 36.

Criminal Papers: SP 44.

Palatinates, comprising the counties of Cheshire, Flint, Durham, and Lancashire.

Chester and Flint

Rough Minute Book: CHES 35/24.

Crown Minute Books: CHES 21/7.

Session Rolls: CHES 24.

Durham

Crown Minute Books: DUR 15/1, 16/1.

Assize Rolls: DUR 17.

Assize Proceedings: DUR 19/3.

Lancaster

Minute Books and Pardons: PL 28/1-3.

Assize Rolls: PL 25.

Indictments: PL 26.

Appendix III

An Act (4 Geo. I, Cap. XI) For the Further Preventing Robbery, Burglary and Other Felonies, and For the More Effectual Transportation of Felons, and Unlawful Exporters of Wool; and For the Declaring the Law upon Some Points Relating to Pirates.

I. Whereas it is found by experience that the punishments inflicted by the laws now in force against the offences of robbery, larceny and other felonious taking and stealing of money and goods, have not proved effectual to deter wicked and evil-disposed persons from being guilty of the said crimes; and whereas many offenders to whom Royal Mercy hath been extended upon condition of transporting themselves to the West Indies have often neglected to perform the said conditions but returned to their former wickedness and been at last for new crimes brought to shameful and ignominious death; and whereas in many of his Majesty's Colonies and Plantations in America there is a great want of servants who, by their labour and industry, might be the means of improving and making the said Colonies and Plantations more useful to this Nation; Be it enacted by the King's most Excellent Majesty, by and with the advice and consent of the Lords Spiritual and Temporal, and the Commons in this present Parliament assembled, and by the authority of the same, that where any person or persons have been convicted of any offence within the benefit of clergy before the twentieth day of January 1717 [/18] and are liable to be whipt or burnt in the hand or have been ordered to any workhouse and who shall be therein on the said twentieth day of January; as also where any person or persons shall be hereafter convicted of grand or petit larceny, or any felonious stealing or taking of money or goods and chattels, either from the person or the house of any other, or in any other manner, and who by the law shall be entitled to the benefit of clergy and liable only to the penalty of burning in the hand or whipping (except persons convicted for receiving or buying stolen goods knowing them to be stolen), it shall and may be lawful for the court before whom they were convicted, or any court held at the same place with the like authority, if they think fit, instead of ordering any such offenders to be burnt in the hand or whipt, to order and direct that such offenders in any workhouse as aforesaid shall be sent as soon as conveniently may be to some of his Majesty's Colonies and Plantations in America for the space of seven years; and that court before whome they were convicted, or any subsequent court held at the same place, with like authority as the former, shall have power to convey, transfer, and make over such offenders by order of court to the use of any person or persons who shall contract for the performance of such transportation, to him or to them, and his and their assigns, for such term of seven years; and where any persons have been convicted, or do now stand attainted of any offences whatsoever, for which death by law ought to be inflicted, or where any offenders shall hereafter be convicted of any crimes whatsoever for which they are by law to be excluded the benefit of clergy, and his Majesty, his Heirs or Successors, shall be graciously pleased to extend Royal Mercy to any such offenders upon the condition of transportation to any part of America, and such intention of mercy be signified by one of his Majesty's Principal Secretaries of State, it shall be and may be lawful to and for any court having proper authority to allow such offenders the benefit of a pardon under the Great Seal, and to order and direct the like transfer and conveyance to any person or persons who will contract for the performance of such transportation, and to his and their assigns, of any such before-mentioned offenders, as also of any person or persons convicted of buying stolen goods, knowing them to be stolen, for the term of fourteen years, in case such condition of transportation be general, or else for such other term or terms as shall be made part of such condition, if any particular time be specified by his Majesty, his Heirs and Successors, as aforesaid, and such person or persons so contracting as aforesaid, his or their assigns, by virtue of such order or transfer as aforesaid, shall have a property and interest in the service of such offenders for such terms of years.

II. And be it further enacted by the authority aforesaid that if any offender or offenders so ordered by any such court to be transported for any term of seven years or fourteen years, or any other time or times as aforesaid, shall return into any part of Great Britain or Ireland before the end of his or their said term, he or she so returning as aforesaid shall be liable to be punished as any person attainted of felony without the benefit of clergy, and execution may and shall be awarded against such offender or offenders accordingly; provided nevertheless that his Majesty, his Heirs and Successors, may at any time pardon and dispense with any such transportation and allow of the return of any such offender or offenders from America, he or they paying their owner or proprietor, at the time of such pardon, dispensation or allowance such sum of money as shall be adjudged reasonable by any two justices of the peace residing within the province where such owner dwells; and where any such offenders shall be transported and shall have served their respective terms, according to the order of any such court as aforesaid, such services shall have the effect of a pardon to all intents and purposes as for that crime or crimes for which they were so transported and shall have so served as aforesaid.

III. And be it further enacted by the authority aforesaid that every such person or persons to whom any court shall order any such offenders to be transferred or conveyed as aforesaid, before any of them shall be delivered over to such person or persons, or his or their assigns, he or they shall contract and agree with any such person or persons as shall be ordered and appointed by such court as aforesaid and give sufficient security, to the satisfaction of such court, that he or they will transport, or cause to be transported, effectually such offenders so conveyed to him or them as aforesaid, to some of his Majesty's Colonies and Plantations in America as shall be ordered by the said court, and procure an authentick certificate from the governor, or the chief custom-house officer of the place (which certificate they are hereby required to give forthwith, without fee or reward, as soon as conveniently may be) of the landing of such offenders so transferred as aforesaid (death and casualties of the sea excepted) and that none of the said offenders shall be suffered to return from the said place to any part of Great Britain or Ireland by the willful default of such person or persons so contracting as aforesaid or by the willful default of his or their assigns.

IV. And whereas there are several persons who have secret acquaintance with felons and who make it their business to help persons to their stolen goods, and by that means gain money from them which is divided between them and the felons, whereby they greatly encourage such offenders, be it enacted by the authority aforesaid that wherever any person taketh money or reward directly or indirectly under pretence or upon account of helping any person or persons to any stolen goods or chattels, every such person so taking money or reward as aforesaid (unless such person doth apprehend or cause to be apprehended such felon who stole the same and cause such felon to be brought to his trial for the same and give evidence against him) shall be guilty of felony and suffer the pains and penalties of felony according to the nature of the felony committed in stealing such goods, and in such and the same manner as if such offender had himself stole such goods and chattels, in the manner and with such circumstances as the same were stolen.

V. And whereas there are many idle persons who are under the age of one and twenty years lurking about in divers parts of London and elsewhere who want employment and may be tempted to become thieves, if not provided for; and whereas they may be inclined to be transported and to enter into services in some of his Majesty's Colonies and Plantations in America, but as they have no power to contract for themselves, and therefore that it is not safe for merchants to transport them or take them into such services; be it enacted by the authority aforesaid that where any person of the age of fifteen years or more, and under the age of twenty one, shall be willing to be transported and to enter into any service in any of his Majesty's Colonies or Plantations in America, it shall and may be lawful for any merchant or other to contract with any such person for any such service not exceeding the term of eight years, provided such person so binding him or herself do come before the Lord Mayor of London, or some other Justice of the Peace of the City, if such contract be made within the same or the liberties thereof, or before some other two Justices of the Peace of the place where such contract shall be made, if made elsewhere, and before such magistrate or magistrates acknowledge such consent and do sign such contract in his or their presence and with his or their approbation, and that then it shall be lawful for any such merchant or other to transport such person so binding him or herself and to keep him or her within any of the said Plantations or Colonies according to the tenor of such contract as aforesaid; and law or statute to the contrary in any wise notwithstanding; which said contract and approbation of such magistrate or magistrates, with the tenor of such contract, shall be certified by such magistrate or magistrates as to the next General Quarter Sessions of the Peace held for that county where such magistrate or magistrates shall reside, to be registered by the Clerk of the Peace without fee or reward.

VI. And be it further enacted by the authority aforesaid that from and after the said twentieth day of January 1717 [/18], if any person or persons shall be in prison for want of sufficient bail for unlawful exportation of wool or woolsels and shall refuse to appear or plead to a declaration or information to be delivered to such person or persons or to the gaoler, keeper or turnkey of the prison, at the said prison, for the said offence by the space of one term, judgment shall be entered against him by default; and in case judgment shall be obtained against any such person or persons by default, verdict, or otherwise, and such person or persons shall not pay the sum recovered against him or them for the said offence within the space of three months after entering up of such judgment, the court before whom such judgment shall be obtained shall, by order of court, cause such offender or offenders to be transported in the same manner as felons aforesaid for the term of seven years; and if such offender or offenders shall return into Great Britain or Ireland before the expiration of the said seven years, he or they shall suffer as felons and have execution awarded against them as persons attainted of felony without benefit of clergy.

VII. [*Clause relating to the suppression of piracy.*]

VIII. Provided always that nothing in this Act contained shall extend or be construed to extend to such persons as shall be convicted or attainted in that part of Great Britain called Scotland.

IX. And be it also enacted that this Act shall extend to all his Majesty's Dominions in America.

Appendix IV

SPECIMENS OF LEGAL DOCUMENTS

Transportation Clause from a Pardon of 1655

Provided nevertheless, and upon this condition, that they the said [*names*] and every of them shalbe, by the Care of our Sherifs of the said County, transported beyond the seas to some English Plantacion with all convenient speed; and if they, or any of them, shall refuse to be transported being thereunto required, or make any escape or retorne in England within tenn yeares after their said Transportation without lawful licence first had, then this our present Pardon to them so refuseing, escapeing or retorning, to be null and voyd.

Contractors' Transportation Bond of 1739

Know all men by these presents that we Jonathan Forward of London, merchant, [*Lord Mayor of London in this year*] and John Whiteing of St. Paul Shadwell in the County of Middlesex, mariner [*master of the transportation ship*], are held and firmly bound to Miles Man Esquire, Common Clerk of the City of London, in One Thousand Six Hundred and Forty Pounds of lawful money of Great Britain to be paid to the said Miles Man or his successors, which payment well and truly to be made, we bind ourselves and each of us, our and each of our heirs, executors and administrators, firmly by these presents sealed with our seals. Dated the twenty second day of January in the Twelfth year of the Reign of our Sovereign Lord George the Second by the Grace of God of Great Britain, France and Ireland, King, Defender of the Faith, and in the year of our Lord 1738.

Whereas at the Sessions of Gaol Delivery of Newgate held for the City of London and County of Middlesex at Justicehall in the Old Bailey the seventeenth day of January instant and at several preceding Sessions [*names of sentenced prisoners*], stand severally convicted of several thefts and larcenys for which they are lyable to the penalty of burning in the Hand or whipping; and whereas his Majesty's Justices of Gaol Delivery of Newgate have ordered and directed that the said [names] and the several other persons abovenamed to be Transported to some of his Majesty's Colonys or plantations in America and to be Transported and Conveyed to such person or persons as shall on or before the thirty first of this Instant January Contract and Agree with the said Miles Man to convey them as soon as conveniently may be to some of his Majesty's Colonys or plantations in America for the Space of Seven years, and the above bounden Jonathan Forward doth hereby Contract and agree to and with the said Miles Man for the performance of such Transportation; now the Condition of this obligation is such that, if the above bounden Jonathan Forward or his assigns do and shall within one month from the day of the date hereof Transport, or cause to be transported, effectually them, the said George Nock and the several other persons above named, for the space of seven years to Maryland or Virginia, being two of his Majesty's Colonys and plantations in America, and do and shall procure an authentick Certificate from the Governor or Chief Customhouse Officer of Maryland or Virginia aforesaid of their landing at Maryland or Virginia aforesaid (Death and Casualtys by Sea excepted) and shall not by their or any of their wilfull default suffer them or any of them to return from Maryland or Virginia aforesaid to any part of Great Britain or Ireland during the said Term of seven years; and if the said Jonathan Forward, his Executors, Administrators or Assigns, shall pay, or Cause to be paid, unto the said Miles Man or his Successors the sum of Forty pounds for every one of them the said George Nock and the several other persons before named whom he, the said Jonathan Forward or his Assigns, shall not Transport to Maryland or Virginia aforesaid within the space of one month, or shall wilfully suffer them or any of them to return to any part of Great Britain or Ireland during the said term of seven years, then this Obligation to be void or else to remain in full Force.

Landing Certificate for Felons of 1719

I, Evan Jones, Deputy Collector of his Majesties Customs in the Port of Annapolis in the Province of Maryland, do hereby Certifie and make known to all persons whom it may or doth Concern, that on the fifth day of this Instant June, Capt. Edwyn Tomkyns, Commander of the *Worcester* ffrigott of London, Burthen 100 Tonns, mounted with 10 Gunns, Navigated with 20 Men, hath transported hither from London and landed the Persons whose names are as follows, the said Capt. Edwyn Tomkyns alledging them to be convicts: [names].

Appendix V

CONVICT SHIPS CONTRACTED FROM
LONDON TO THE AMERICAN COLONIES 1716-1775

This list comprises all the ships contracted to the justices of London, Middlesex and the Home Counties to carry convicts from London, Middlesex and the Home Counties. See Appendix VI for details of convict ships contracted by justices outside this jurisdiction.

Sailing	Name of Ship	Master	Destination	Reference
Dec 1716	Lewis	Roger Laming	Jamaica	T53/25/224
Jan 1717	Queen Elizabeth		Jamaica	T53/25/225
May 1718	Unknown		Barbados & Antigua	Bond
May 1718	Tryal		S. Carolina	Bond
Aug 1718	Eagle[1]	Robt. Staples	S. Carolina*	T53/27/36
Feb 1719	Worcester	Edwin Tomkins	Maryland*	T53/27/220
May 1719	Margaret	Wm. Greenwood	Maryland*	T53/27/266
Oct 1719	Susannah & Sarah	Peter Wills	Maryland*	T53/27/415
May 1720	Honor[2]	Robt. Russell	Virginia*	T53/28/157
Oct 1720	Gilbert	Darby Lux	Maryland*	T53/28/331
Aug 1721	Prince Royal	Thos. Boyd	Virginia*	T53/29/146
Aug 1721	Owners Goodwill	John Lux	Maryland*	T53/29/147
Oct 1721	William & John	John Thompson	Maryland	T53/29/453
Jan 1722	Gilbert	Darby Lux	Maryland*	T53/29/451
Feb 1722	Christabella	Amb. Griffin	Jamaica	Bond
Jly 1722	Alexander	John Graham	Nevis*	T53/29/531
Oct 1722	Forward	Daniel Russell	Maryland*	T53/30/118
Feb 1723	Jonathan[3]	Darby Lux	Maryland*	T53/30/341
May 1723	Victory	Wm. Wharton	W. Indies	T53/30/339
Jly 1723	Alexander	John King	Maryland*	T53/30/340
Oct 1723	Forward	Daniel Russell	Virginia	T53/30/453
Feb 1724	Anne[4]	Thos. Wrangham	Carolina	T53/31/77
Jly 1724	Robert	John Vickers	Maryland*	T53/31/255
Oct 1724	Forward[5]	Daniel Russell	Maryland*	T53/31/376
Dec 1724	Rappahannock Mcht.[6]	John Jones	Virginia	T53/31/376
Apr 1725	Sukey	John Ellis	Maryland*	T53/32/93
Sep 1725	Forward	Dan. Russell	Maryland*	T53/32/219
Nov 1725	Rappahannock Mcht.	Chas. Whale	Virginia*	T53/32/220
Feb 1726	Supply	John Rendell	Maryland*	T53/32/385
Jun 1726	Loyal Margaret	John Wheaton	Maryland*	T53/32/386
Oct 1726	Forward	Dan. Russell	Virginia	T53/33/294
Mar 1727	Rappahannock Mcht.	Chas. Whale	Maryland	T53/33/296
Jly 1727	Susanna	John Vickers	Virginia	T53/33/364
Sep 1727	Forward	Wm. Loney	Virginia*	Bond
Dec 1727	Unknown	Wm. Williams	Unknown	Bond
May 1728	Unknown	Sam. Waller	New York	Bond
Jun 1728	Elizabeth	Wm. Whithome	Virginia*	T53/34/154
Nov 1728	Forward	Wm. Loney	Virginia*	T53/34/303

Sailing	Name of Ship	Master	Destination	Reference
Mar 1729	Patapsco Merchant	Darby Lux	Maryland*	T53/34/418
Nov 1729	Forward	Wm. Loney	Virginia*	T53/35/43
Mar 1730	Patapsco Merchant	Darby Lux	Maryland*	T53/35/174
Sep 1730	Smith	Wm. Loney	Virginia	T53/35/379
Nov 1730	Forward	Geo. Buckeridge	Virginia*	T53/35/380
Mar 1731	Patapsco Merchant	Darby Lux	Maryland*	T53/35/496
Apr 1731	Bennett	James Reed	Virginia	T53/35/498
Oct 1731	Smith	Wm. Loney	Virginia*	T53/36/138
Dec 1731	Forward	Geo. Buckeridge	Virginia	T53/36/212
Apr 1732	Patapsco Merchant	Darby Lux	Maryland*	T53/36/306
Oct 1732	Caesar	Wm. Loney	Virginia*	T53/36/424
Feb 1733	Smith	Geo. Buckeridge	Maryland or Va.	T53/37/10
Apr 1733	Patapsco Merchant	Darby Lux	Maryland*	T53/37/11
Jan 1734	Caesar	Wm. Loney	Virginia*	T53/37/212
Apr 1734	Patapsco Merchant	Darby Lux	Maryland	T53/37/304
Dec 1734	Caesar	Wm. Loney	Virginia*	T53/37/446
Apr 1735	Patapsco Merchant	Darby Lux	Maryland*	T53/38/80
Dec 1735	John	John Griffin	Maryland*	T53/38/255
Feb 1736	Dorsetshire	Wm. Loney	Virginia*	T53/38/256
May 1736	Patapsco Merchant	Francis Lux	Maryland	T53/38/337
Dec 1736	Dorsetshire	Wm. Loney	Virginia	T53/38/456
May 1737	Forward	John Magier	Virginia	T53/39/123
Sep 1737	Pretty Patsy	Francis Lux	Maryland	T53/39/121
Jan 1738	Dorsetshire	John Whiting	Virginia	T53/39/182
Jun 1738	Forward	John Magier	Virginia or Md.	T53/39/248
Oct 1738	Genoa	Darby Lux	Maryland	T53/39/409
Jan 1739	Dorsetshire	John Whiting	Virginia	T53/39/408
Apr 1739	Forward	Ben. Richardson	Virginia	T53/39/448
Jly 1739	Sea Nymph	Adam Muir of Md.	Maryland	Bond
Oct 1739	Duke of Cumberland	Wm. Harding	Virginia	T53/40/45
Feb 1740	York	Anthony Bacon	Maryland	T53/40/170
Jun 1740	Essex	Ambrose Cock	Maryland or Va.	T53/40/204
Jan 1741	Vernon	Henry Lee	Maryland	T53/40/289
Jan 1741	Harpooner	John Wilson	Virginia	T53/40/290
Apr 1741	Speedwell	Wm. Camplin	Maryland	T53/40/337
Apr 1741	Mediterranean	Geo. Harriot	Maryland	T53/40/338
May 1741	Cath. & Elizabeth	Wm. Chapman	Maryland	T53/40/338
Aug 1741	Sally	Wm. Napier	Maryland	T53/40/415
Oct 1741	Sea Horse	John Rendell	Virginia	T53/40/414
Feb 1742	Industry	Chas. Barnard	Maryland	T53/40/484
Apr 1742	Bond	John Gardiner	Maryland	T53/40/485
Jun 1742	Bladon	Samuel Laurence	Maryland	T53/41/129
Sep 1742	Forward[7]	John Sargent	America	T53/41/130
Apr 1743	Justitia[8]	Barnet Bond	America	T53/41/227
Apr 1743	Bond	Matthew Johnson	America	T53/41/326
May 1743	Indian Queen	Edward Maxwell	Maryland	T53/41/326
Nov 1743	George William	Jack Campbell	America	T53/41/327
Feb 1744	Neptune	James Knight	Maryland	T53/41/419
May 1744	Justitia	Jack Campbell	America	T53/41/462
Oct 1744	Savannah	James Dobbins	America	T53/42/64
May 1745	?Tryal	John Johnstoun	America	Mddx Bond
Jly 1745	Italian Merchant	Alexander Reid	America	T53/42/220
Jan 1746	Plain Dealer[9]	James Dobbins	America	T53/42/220
Apr 1746	Laura	William Gracie	America	T53/42/220

Appendix V

Sailing	Name of Ship	Master	Destination	Reference
Sep 1746	Mary[10]	John Johnstoun	America	T53/42/335
Jan 1747	George William	James Dobbins	America	T53/42/335
Jly 1747	Laura	William Gracie	America	T53/42/427
Jan 1748	St. George	James Dobbins	Maryland	T53/42/519
Jan 1748	Laura	William Gracie	America	T1/330/55
Jun 1748	Lichfield	John Johnstoun	America	T53/43/101
Jly 1748	*Unknown*	John Ramsey	America	Mddx Bond
Jan 1749	Laura	William Gracie	America	T53/43/190
May 1749	Lichfield	John Johnstoun	America	T53/43/273
Aug 1749	Thames	James Dobbins	America	T53/43/320
Nov 1749	Mary	Leonard Gerrard	America	T53/43/320
Apr 1750	Tryal	John Johnstoun	America	T1/340/20
May 1750	Lichfield	William Gracie	America	T1/340/33
Oct 1750	Rachael	John Armstrong	America	T1/342/35
Jan 1751	Thames	James Dobbins	America	T53/44/63
May 1751	Tryal	John Johnstoun	America	T1/346/29
Sep 1751	Greyhound	William Gracie	America	T1/349/1
Feb 1752	Thames	James Dobbins	America	T53/44/243
May 1752	Lichfield	Leonard Gerrard	America	T1/348/8
Aug 1752	Tryal	John Johnstoun	America	T53/44/379
Dec 1752	Greyhound	William Gracie	America	T1/348/26
Apr 1753	Thames	James Dobbins	America	T1/351/17
Jly 1753	Tryal	John Johnstoun	America	T1/353/29
Dec 1753	Whiteing	Matt. Johnson	America	T1/358/1
Mar 1754	Thames	James Dobbins	America	T53/45/116
Jun 1754	Tryal	Isaac Johns	America	T53/45/116
Oct 1754	Ruby	Edward Ogle	America	T53/45/117
Feb 1755	Greyhound	Alex. Stewart	arr. Md. Apr 1755	T53/45/117, CO5/750
May 1755	Rose	Thomas Slade	America	T1/361/39
Sep 1755	Tryal	Wm. McGachin	America	T1/361/67
Jan 1756	Greyhound	Alex. Stewart	arr. Md. Apr 1756	T1/367/2, CO5/750
Jun 1756	Lyon	James Dyer	America	T1/365/98
Oct 1756	Barnard	Philip Weatherall	America	T53/45/575
Mar 1757	Tryal	Alex. Scott	America	T53/46/110
Sep 1757	Thetis	James Edmonds	arr. Maryland Dec.	T1/378/64, CO5/750
Mar 1758	Dragon	Wm. McGachin	America	T1/387/17
Sep 1758	Tryal	George Freebaim	arr. Md. Jan 1759	T1/387/29, CO5/750
Dec 1758	The Brothers	Allan Boyd	America	T1/390/156
Feb 1759	?Dragon	Wm. McGachin	America	Mddx Bond
Apr 1759	Thetis	Matthew Craymer	America	T1/391
Dec 1759	Phoenix	Dougal McDougal	America	T1/397/15
Mar 1760	Friendship	Dougal McDougal	America	T1/401
Apr 1760	Thetis	Matthew Craymer	America	T1/401
Oct 1760	Phoenix	Wm. McGachin	America	T53/47/56
Mar 1761	Neptune	Benjamin Dawson	America	T53/47/56
Apr 1761	Dolphin	Dougal McDougal	America	T53/47/56
Oct 1761	Maryland	Alex. Ramsay	America	T53/47/57
Apr 1762	Dolphin	Matt. Craymer	Maryland	T1/418
Apr 1762	Neptune	Ben. Dawson	America	T1/418
Nov 1762	Prince William	Dougal McDougal	America	T1/418

Emigrants in Chains

Sailing	Name of Ship	Master	Destination	Reference
Mar 1763	Neptune	Colin Somervell	America	T1/423
May 1763	Dolphin	Matt. Craymer	Maryland	T53/48/57
Aug 1763	Beverly	Robert Allan	Virginia	T53/49/136
Dec 1763	Neptune	Colin Somervell	Maryland	T1/423
Mar 1764	Tryal	Wm. McGachin	America	T1/429
Jun 1764	Dolphin	Dougal McDougal	America	T1/429
Sep 1764	Justitia	Colin Somervell	America	T1/429
Jan 1765	Tryal	John Errington	America	T1/437
Apr 1765	Ann	Christopher Reed	America	T1/437
Sep 1765	Justitia	Colin Somervell	America	T1/437
Jan 1766	Tryal	John Errington	America	T1/449
Apr 1766	Ann	Chris. Reed	America	T1/449
Oct 1766	Justitia	Colin Somervell	arr. Va. November	T1/450, CO5/1450
Jan 1767	Tryal	John Somervell	America	T53/50/93
May 1767	Thornton	Chris. Reed	Maryland	T1/460/4
Sep 1767	Justitia	Colin Somervell	America	T1/456
Dec 1767	*Unknown*	John Gill	America	Bond
Jan 1768	Neptune	James Arbuckle	America	T1/465
Apr 1768	Thornton	Chris. Reed	America	T1/465
Jun 1768	Tryal	Dougal McDougal	America	T1/465
Oct 1768	Justitia	Colin Somervell	America	T1/465
Feb 1769	Thornton	Chris. Reed	Maryland	T1/470
May 1769	Tryal	Dougal McDougal	America	T53/51/132
Sep 1769	Douglas	Wm. Beckenridge	America	T1/470
Feb 1770	Justitia	Colin Somervell	America	T1/478
Apr 1770	New Tryal	Dougal McDougal	Maryland	T1/478
Jly 1770	Scarsdale	Chris. Reed	America	T1/478
Dec 1770	Justitia	Colin Somervell	America	T1/483
May 1771	Thornton	Dougal McDougal	America	T1/483
Jly 1771	Scarsdale	Chris. Reed	America	T1/483
Jan 1772	Justitia	Neil Gillis	America	T1/483
Apr 1772	Thornton	John Kidd	America	T1/490
Jly 1772	Orange Bay	Neil Somerville	America	T1/490
Sailing	Name of Ship	Master	Destination	Reference
Jly 1772	Tayloe	Dougal McDougal	America	T1/490
Jan 1773	Justitia	Finlay Gray	America	Mddx Bond
Mar 1773	?Thornton	John Kidd	America	Mddx Bond
May 1773	Hanover Planter	Wm. McCulloch	America	Mddx Bond
Jly 1773	Tayloe	John Ogilvy	Virginia	Mddx Bond
Jan 1774	*Unknown*	Finlay Gray	America	Mddx Bond
Apr 1774	?Thornton	John Kidd	America	Mddx Bond
Jly 1774	?Green Garland	John Ogilvy	America	Mddx Bond
Jan 1775	Justitia	John Kidd	arr. Virginia Mar	Mddx Bond
Apr 1775	Thornton	Finlay Gray	America	Mddx Bond
Jly 1775	Saltspring	John Ogilvy	Maryland	Mddx Bond
Oct 1775	*Unknown*	John Kidd	America	Mddx Bond

* Indicates that Landing Certificates survive in Corporation of London Records Office.

NOTES

1. The *Eagle* was formerly employed in the black slave trade (PRO: C11/1094/23).

2. Fifteen felons on board the *Honour* mutinied and forced her captain to put them ashore at Vigo.

3. The *Jonathan* was also a former black slaver (PRO: C11/1400/2) which caught fire and sank in Maryland in June 1724 (PRO: C11/2581/8).

4. The *Anne* was a black slaver between 1717 and 1720.

5. A contingent of convicts from Lincolnshire who were designated to embark on this ship escaped (PRO: C11/260/69). Many were subsequently rounded up and loaded on to another ship where most perished.

6. Captain Jones died of smallpox when his ship reached Falmouth. The convicts aboard were heavily infected with "gaol fever" and thirty-eight of them died before journey's end (PRO: C11/1223/28).

7. When she arrived at Potomac fifty-eight of the seventy-four convicts embarked in London were found to have died. Captain Sargent was indicted in 1744 for offences committed against his passengers but was discharged (PRO: HCA 1/20/5). On her homeward voyage the *Forward* was taken prize by a Spanish privateer (PRO: C11/2499/9).

8. Captain Bond was also indicted in 1744 for murder and robbery on the high seas, and was also acquitted (PRO: HCA 1/20/5).

9. The *Plain Dealer* fought an engagement with the French *Zephyre* in which the convicts fought valiantly before their ship was wrecked on the French coast with the loss of most on board.

10. This ship appears to have been lost at sea. (Papers in Middlesex Records.)

Appendix VI

CONVICT SHIPS CONTRACTED BY
ASSIZE AND QUARTER SESSION COURTS*

Sailing	Port	Name of Ship	Master	Destination	Reference
Nov 1671	?London	Elizabeth	?	arr. Md. Feb 1672	Md. Land Books
Apr 1721	*Unknown*	Mary	John Friend	arr. Va. Jun 1721	Bond
Apr 1735	Liverpool	Squire	?	arr. Md. Aug 1735	Derbys. records
Jan 1736	Liverpool	Squire	?	arr. Md. Apr 1736	Derbys. records
Apr 1742	Liverpool	Shaw	?	arr. Md. Jun 1742	Derbys. records
Apr 1742	London	Samuel	John Everard	Maryland	E134/26 Geo 2/Trin 5[1]
Feb 1743	Liverpool	Shaw	?	arr. Md. May 1743	Derbys. records
1746	*Unknown*	William & Anne	?	arr. Md. Aug 1746	*NGSQ*
Aug 1751	Liverpool	Happy Jennett	?	arr. Md. Oct 1751	Derbys. records
1752	London	Nightingale	John Lancey	Maryland	*Tyburn Chronicle*
Aug 1754	Bristol	Bideford	John Cole	arr. Md. Dec 1754	CO5/750
Jan 1755	Bristol	Greyhound	Alex Stewart	arr. Md. Apr 1756	CO5/750
Apr 1756	London	Lux	?	arr. Md. Jun 1756	CO5/750
Apr 1757	London	Lux	?	?Maryland	Sheriffs' Cravings
Jun 1757	London	Thomas & Sarah	?	arr. Md. Jly 1757	CO5/750
May 1757	Bristol	Frisby	?	Maryland	*Bristol Intelligencer*
Oct 1757	Bristol	Betsey	Wm. Strachan	arr. Md. Dec 1757	CO5/750
Apr 1758	Bideford	Peace	Thos. Lovering	arr. Md. Jun 1758	CO5/750
Apr 1758	Bristol	Eugene	Jonathan Tallimay	arr. Md. Jun 1758	CO5/750
Sep 1758	Bristol	Betsey	Wm. Strachan	arr. Md. Nov 1758	CO5/750
Sep 1758	London	Lux	— Wilcocks	Baltimore	Sheriffs' Cravings
Apr 1759	Bideford	Maryland Mcht.	Thos. Spencer	arr. Md. Jun 1759	CO5/750
Oct 1759	London	Mary	Thos. Gray	arr. Va. Jan 1760	CO5/1448
Oct 1761	London	British King	Thos. Gray	arr. Va. Jan 1762	CO5/1448
May 1762	London	Sally	?	arr. Md. Jun 1762	*Sufferings of W.G.*
Sep 1762	Bideford	Betsey	Nich. Andrew	arr. Md. Nov 1762	CO5/750
1763	Bristol	Albion	John Cole	arr. Md. Aug 1763	*NGSQ*
Sep 1763	?Bristol	Betsey	Nich. Andrew	arr. Md. Nov 1763	
Apr 1764	Bristol	Little Nancy	W. Temple	arr. Va. Jun 1764	CO5/1450
1764	?London	Neptune	Colin Somervell	arr. Md. 1764	*NGSQ*
1765	Bristol	Albion	Thos. Spencer	arr. Md. 1765	*NGSQ*
Jan 1765	Hull	Ann	Richd. Dowdall	arr. Va. Mar 1765	CO5/1450
Apr 1765	Liverpool	Young Samuel	Joseph Kendall	arr. Va. Jun 1765	CO5/1449
Sep 1765	Whitehaven	Lady Walpole	Edwd. Davidson	arr. Va. Nov 1765	CO5/1449
1768	?Newcastle	Rodney	?	wrecked on Antigua	*Gentleman's Mag*[2]
1769	?Bristol	Isabella	?	arr. Md. Jly 1769	*NGSQ*
Jly 1771	Bristol	Restoration	Capt. Thomas	arr. Md. Oct. 1771	*NGSQ*
Jly 1774	?London	Aston Hall	John Parker	arr. Md. Sep 1774	*NGSQ*
Sep 1775	London	Rebecca	— Brown	Baltimore	Sheriffs' Cravings
Jan 1776	?Newcastle	Jenney	?	arr. Va. Apr 1776	*Va. Gazette*

179

NOTES

*This list is very far from complete and contains notes derived from occasional references in official documents.

1. Captured by Spanish privateer.

2. Bound for Maryland with a cargo of convicts, she was driven to Antigua and wrecked. The survivors were reduced to eating their shoes to survive. (See *Gentleman's Magazine* for May 1768.)

Appendix VII

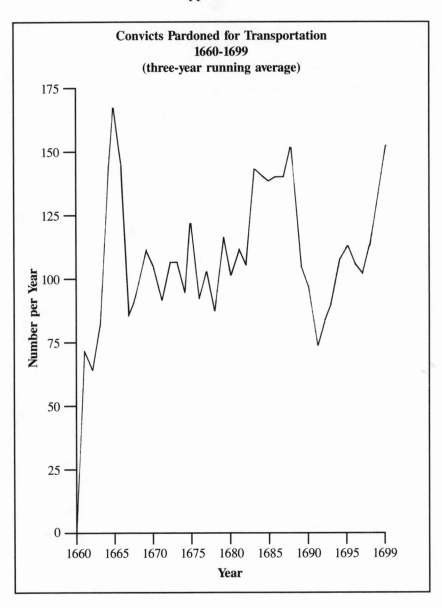

Appendix VIII

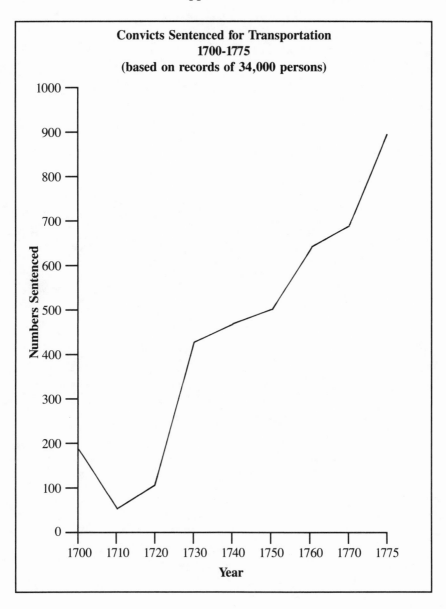

Convicts Sentenced for Transportation
1700-1775
(based on records of 34,000 persons)

Appendix IX

BENJAMIN FRANKLIN
ON THE SUBJECT OF TRANSPORTATION

The following letter, widely attributed to Benjamin Franklin, appeared in the *Pennsylvania Gazette* of 9 May 1751. The text was reprinted in *The Nation* of 1 September 1898.

By a passage in one of your late Papers I understand that the Government at home will not suffer our mistaken Assemblies to make any law for preventing or discouraging the importation of convicts from Great Britain for this kind reason: "That such Laws are against the public utility as they tend to prevent the IMPROVEMENT and WELL PEOPLING of the Colonies."

Such a tender parental concern in our Mother Country for the welfare of her children calls aloud for the highest returns of gratitude and duty. This everyone must be sensible of. But 'tis said that, in our present circumstances, it is absolutely impossible for us to make such as are adequate to the favour. I own it, but nevertheless let us do our endeavour.

In some of the uninhabited parts of these Provinces there are numbers of those venomous reptiles we call rattlesnakes: felons-convict from the beginning of the world. These, whenever we meet with them, we put to death by virtue of an old law, "Thou shalt bruise his head." But, as this is a sanguinary law and may seem too cruel, and as however mischievous these creatures are with us, they may possibly change their natures if they were to change the climate, I would humbly propose that this general sentence of death be changed for transportation.

In the Spring of the year, when they first creep out of their holes, they are feeble, heavy, slow, and easily taken: and if a small bounty were allowed per head, some thousands might be collected annually and transported to Britain. There I would propose to have them carefully distributed in St. James's Park, in the Spring Gardens, and in other places of pleasure about London; in the gardens of all the nobility and gentry throughout the nation, but particularly in the gardens of the Prime Ministers, the Lords of Trade and Members of Parliament: for to them we are most particularly obliged.

185

There is no human scheme so perfect but some inconveniences may be objected to it. Yet, when the conveniences far exceed, the scheme is judged rational and fit to be executed. Thus inconveniences have been objected to that *good* and *wise* Act of Parliament by virtue of which all the Newgates and dungeons in Britain are emptied into the Colonies. It has been said that these thieves and villains introduced among us spoil the morals of youth in the neighbourhoods that entertain them and perpetrate many horrid crimes. But let not private interests obstruct public utility. Our Mother knows what is best for us. What is a little house-breaking, shop-lifting, or highway robbery; what is a son now and then corrupted and hanged; a daughter debauched and poxed, a wife stabbed, a husband's throat cut, or a child's brains beat out with an axe, compared with this IMPROVEMENT and WELL PEOPLING of the Colonies?

Thus it may, perhaps, be objected to my scheme that the rattlesnake is a mischievous creature, and that changing his nature with the clime is a mere supposition not yet confirmed by sufficient facts. What then? Is not example more prevalent than precept? And may not the honest, rough British Gentry, by a familiarity with these reptiles, learn to creep, and to insinuate, and to slaver, and to wriggle into Place (and perhaps to poison such as stand in their way), qualities of no small advantage to courtiers? In comparison of which *Improvement* and *Public Utility* what is a child now and then killed by their venomous bite . . . or even a favourite lap-dog?

I would only add that this exporting of felons to the Colonies may be considered as a trade as well as in the light of a favour. Now all commerce implies returns; justice requires them; there can be no trade without them. And rattlesnakes seem the most suitable returns for the human serpents sent us by our Mother Country. In this, however, as in every other branch of trade, She will have the advantage of us. She will reap equal benefits without equal risk of the inconveniences and dangers. For the rattlesnake gives warning before he attempts his mischief, which the convict does not.

I am,

Yours etc.

Americanus

SELECT BIBLIOGRAPHY

Blumenthal, Walter Hart. *Brides from Bridewell*. Rutland, Vt.: Tuttle Press, 1962.

Butler, James Davie. "British Convicts Shipped to the American Colonies." *American Historical Review* 2 (1896): 12 ff.

Coldham, Peter Wilson. "Transportation of English Felons." *National Genealogical Society Quarterly* 63 (1975): 172 ff.

_____. *The Complete Book of Emigrants in Bondage 1614-1775*. Baltimore: Genealogical Publishing Co., 1988.

Craies, William F. "The Compulsion of Subjects to Leave the Realm." *Law Quarterly Review* 6 (1890): 398 ff.

Ekirch, A. Roger. "Great Britain's Secret Convict Trade to America 1783-1784." *American Historical Review* 89 (1984): 1285 ff.

_____. "Bound for America: A Profile of British Convicts Transported to the Colonies, 1718-1775." *William and Mary Quarterly*, Third Series, 42 (1985): 184-200.

_____. *Bound for America: The Transportation of British Convicts to the Colonies 1718-1775*. Oxford: Clarendon Press, 1987.

Eltis, D. "Free and Coerced Transatlantic Migrations: Some Comparisons." *American Historical Review* 88 (1983): 251 ff.

Harrison, Fairfax. "When the Convicts Came." *Virginia Magazine of History and Biography* 30 (1922): 250 ff.

Kaminkow, M. and J. *Original Lists of Emigrants in Bondage from London to the American Colonies 1718-1744*. Baltimore: Magna Carta Book Co., 1967.

Lang, John Dunmore. *Transportation and Colonization*. London, 1837.

Mackeson, John F. *Bristol Transported*. Bristol: Redcliffe Press, 1987.

Morgan, Kenneth. "The Organisation of the Convict Trade to Maryland 1768-1775." *William and Mary Quarterly*, Third Series, 42 (1985): 201-227.

_____. "English and American Attitudes Towards Convict Transportation 1718-1775." *History* 72 (1987): 416-431.

Oldham, Wilfrid. *Britain's Convicts to the Colonies*. Sydney: Library of Australian History, 1990.

Shaw, A.G.L. *Convicts and the Colonies: A Study of Penal Transportation*. London: Faber, 1966.

Smith, Abbot E. "The Transportation of Criminals to the American Colonies in the Seventeenth Century." *American Historical Review* 39 (1934): 232 ff.

_____. *Colonists in Bondage: White Servitude and Convict Labor in America 1607-1776.* Chapel Hill: University of Carolina Press, 1947.

Sollers, Basil. "Transported Convict Laborers in Maryland During the Colonial Period." *Maryland Historical Magazine* 2 (1907): 17-47.

Wyatt, J. W. "Transportation from Gloucestershire, 1718-1773." *Gloucestershire Historical Studies* 3 (1969): 2-16.